Beyond the language classroom: researching MOOCs and other innovations

Edited by Kan Qian and Stephen Bax

Published by Research-publishing.net, not-for-profit association
Dublin, Ireland; Voillans, France, info@research-publishing.net

© 2017 by Editors (collective work)
© 2017 by Authors (individual work)

Beyond the language classroom: researching MOOCs and other innovations
Edited by Kan Qian and Stephen Bax

Rights: This volume is published under the Attribution-NonCommercial-NoDerivatives International (CC BY-NC-ND) licence; **individual articles may have a different licence**. Under the CC BY-NC-ND licence, the volume is freely available online (https://doi.org/10.14705/rpnet.2017.mooc2016.9781908416537) for anybody to read, download, copy, and redistribute provided that the author(s), editorial team, and publisher are properly cited. Commercial use and derivative works are, however, not permitted.

Disclaimer: Research-publishing.net does not take any responsibility for the content of the pages written by the authors of this book. The authors have recognised that the work described was not published before, or that it was not under consideration for publication elsewhere. While the information in this book are believed to be true and accurate on the date of its going to press, neither the editorial team, nor the publisher can accept any legal responsibility for any errors or omissions that may be made. The publisher makes no warranty, expressed or implied, with respect to the material contained herein. While Research-publishing.net is committed to publishing works of integrity, the words are the authors' alone.

Trademark notice: product or corporate names may be trademarks or registered trademarks, and are used only for identification and explanation without intent to infringe.

Copyrighted material: every effort has been made by the editorial team to trace copyright holders and to obtain their permission for the use of copyrighted material in this book. In the event of errors or omissions, please notify the publisher of any corrections that will need to be incorporated in future editions of this book.

Typeset by Research-publishing.net
Cover design and cover photos by © Raphaël Savina (raphael@savina.net)

ISBN13: 978-1-908416-52-0 (Paperback - Print on demand, black and white)
Print on demand technology is a high-quality, innovative and ecological printing method; with which the book is never 'out of stock' or 'out of print'.

ISBN13: 978-1-908416-53-7 (Ebook, PDF, colour)
ISBN13: 978-1-908416-54-4 (Ebook, EPUB, colour)

Legal deposit, Ireland: The National Library of Ireland, The Library of Trinity College, The Library of the University of Limerick, The Library of Dublin City University, The Library of NUI Cork, The Library of NUI Maynooth, The Library of University College Dublin, The Library of NUI Galway.

Legal deposit, United Kingdom: The British Library.
British Library Cataloguing-in-Publication Data.
A cataloguing record for this book is available from the British Library.

Legal deposit, France: Bibliothèque Nationale de France - Dépôt légal: juin 2017.

Table of contents

v   Notes on contributors

1   Introduction to Beyond the language classroom: researching MOOCs and other innovations
Kan Qian and Stephen Bax

5   Internationalization of higher education and the use of MOOCs to improve second language proficiency: the MOVE-ME project
Donatella Troncarelli and Andrea Villarini

15   Researching into a MOOC embedded flipped classroom model for college English Reading and Writing course
Zhang Xinying

29   The MOOC-CLIL project: using MOOCs to increase language, and social and online learning skills for 5th grade K-12 students
Inge de Waard and Kathy Demeulenaere

43   Dualism-based design of the Introductory Chinese MOOC 'Kit de contact en langue chinoise'
Jue Wang-Szilas and Joël Bellassen

59   The Move-Me project: reflecting on xMOOC and cMOOC structure and pedagogical implementation
Laura McLoughlin and Francesca Magnoni

71   Integrating a MOOC into the postgraduate ELT curriculum: reflecting on students' beliefs with a MOOC blend
Marina Orsini-Jones, Barbara Conde Gafaro, and Shooq Altamimi

85   MOOCs for language learning – opportunities and challenges: the case of the Open University Italian Beginners' MOOCs
Anna Motzo and Anna Proudfoot

Table of contents

99 An exploration of the use of mobile applications to support the learning of Chinese characters employed by students of Chinese as a foreign language
Amanda Mason and Zhang Wenxin

113 English at your fingertips: learning initiatives for rural areas
Lilit Bekaryan, Zaruhi Soghomonyan, and Arusyak Harutyunyan

127 The language exchange programme: plugging the gap in formal learning
Tita Beaven, Mara Fuertes Gutiérrez, and Anna Motzo

141 Informal learning activities for learners of English and for learners of Dutch
Anne Van Marsenille

153 Author index

Notes on contributors

Editors

Kan Qian[1] is a senior lecturer in the School of Languages and Applied Linguistics, The Open University (UK). Her research focuses on the use of technologies for the learning and teaching of languages: mobile language learning, app-assisted informal Chinese language learning, interactions in online discussion forums, and online language learning design, including MOOC design.

Stephen Bax is a professor of Modern Languages and Linguistics and Director of Research Excellence in the School of Languages and Applied Linguistics, The Open University (UK). His research includes work on the normalisation of new technologies in language education, and he was awarded the 2014 TESOL Distinguished Researcher Award for his research using eye tracking technology in investigating reading. He has recently developed an online tool for analysing lexis in text, textinspector.com, which was shortlisted for the international British Council ELTons awards for Digital Innovation 2017.

Authors

Shooq Altamimi is a teacher education specialist at the Directorate of Training and Development at the Ministry of Education in the Kingdom of Bahrain. Altamimi graduated from Bahrain Teachers College, University of Bahrain, with a Bachelor of Education. She received her Master of Arts in English Language Teaching with Distinction in 2016 from Coventry University. She participated in a telecollaboration project with Bogazici University, Turkey, and gave several talks with other students and staff regarding her learning experience, MOOCs, and Threshold Concepts in Turkey and in the UK. Her research interests include teacher education, threshold concepts, telecollaboration, and autonomous learning.

---

1. Kan is the surname.

Notes on contributors

Tita Beaven is a senior lecturer in Spanish at the School of Languages and Applied Linguistics at The Open University (UK). Her research is in the area of innovative pedagogy and technology in language learning and teaching and open education. She holds a Doctorate in Education (Educational Technology) from The Open University.

Lilit Bekaryan has a fifteen-year experience in teaching, ranging from teaching teenagers to adults. At present, she teaches at university level, provides teacher training and mentoring services, and teaches a course of "English for the Media" to journalists, a project funded by the US Embassy in Yerevan. Her professional interests include curriculum design, classroom management, and assessment. Her prior expertise includes course development and virtual instruction. She earned her PhD in English Philology and Social Psychology. Her teaching qualifications include CELTA and DELTA, international teaching awards issued by the University of Cambridge.

Joël Bellassen holds a HDR (Habilitation à Diriger des Recherches) in 1997 and is a PhD supervisor of INALCO (Paris, France). He was the first General Inspector of Chinese Language Teaching nominated by the Ministry of National Education (France). He has published more than one hundred books, articles, as well as audio-visual teaching materials in the field of Teaching Chinese as a Foreign Language. He is the author of the first Chinese language syllabus for French secondary schools. His current research interests include teaching of Chinese as a second language, history of Chinese education, and evaluation of Chinese teaching materials.

Barbara Conde Gafaro is an English language teacher from Colombia. She obtained her Bachelor Degree in Modern Languages at the Pontificia Javeriana University in Bogota, Colombia. Her thesis was published in the Lingua Xaveriana Journal by the faculty of Communication and Language. In 2017, she obtained distinction for her dissertation on a blended MOOC integration for the MA in English Language Teaching and Applied Linguistics at Coventry University where she currently works as a Spanish lecturer and research assistant for the B-MELTT British Council project (Blending MOOCs for English Language Teacher Training).

Inge de Waard (PhD) has an extensive research background in investigating and implementing Innovative Educational Technologies (The Open University, UK; EIT InnoEnergy, EU; Institute of Tropical Medicine, Belgium; Athabasca University, Canada). She has set-up, coordinated and developed several online and mobile learning projects, always with a focus on participation and durability. These projects involved partners and individuals from both the Northern (Canada, United States, Italy, Belgium, Ireland, Germany, UK) and Southern regions (South-Africa, India, Peru, Morocco).

Kathy Demeulenaere is a language teacher at the Guldensporencollege (GUSCO) in Kortrijk, Belgium. In the past she has been involved in several innovative language projects for K12 students combining innovative pedagogical approaches.

Mara Fuertes Gutiérrez is a lecturer in Spanish at the School of Languages and Applied Linguistics at The Open University (UK). She holds a PhD in Spanish Linguistics from the Universidad de Valladolid (Spain) and her current research interests are in the field of innovative pedagogy and linguistic theories applied to language learning and teaching.

Arusyak Harutyunyan teaches ESP classes at the International Scientific-Educational Center of National Academy of Sciences, Armenia. She is a CELTA certified ESL tutor and has a Cambridge CPE certificate. Being an advocate for open knowledge, she was the first to design and teach language-learning MOOCs in Armenia. Her interests range from ESP, learning technologies, to quality assurance. She is currently doing her PhD on teaching legal English vocabulary in online and offline learning environments.

Francesca Magnoni is part-time lecturer at Italian Studies in NUI Galway. She has a PhD in Foreign Language Teaching and Learning and a ten year experience of teaching Italian as a foreign language in English speaking countries and teaching English in Italy. Her research interests lie in the field of Pedagogy of Foreign Languages, with a special focus on the use of hypertexts in language learning and teaching, on online language courses, and LMOOCs development.

Amanda Mason has a background in English as a Foreign Language (EFL) and Teaching English to Speakers of Other Languages (TESOL), and has been working with international students for over 20 years. Her interest in Chinese began ten years ago when she enrolled on a beginner's class in order to be able to pronounce her Chinese students' names. Since then, she has been questioning the extent to which the perceived wisdom from EFL learning and teaching can be applied to learning Chinese as a foreign language and Chinese-speaking EFL learners. Her other main research interest is the internationalisation of higher education.

Laura McLoughlin, PhD, is lecturer at the National University of Ireland, Galway, co-Director of the MA in Advanced Language Skills, Coordinator of the Diploma in Italian Online. Her research interests include Applied Linguistics, Audiovisual Translation, and CALL. She is the recipient of several international funding awards, and the winner of three European Language Labels. A list of recent publications can be found here (http://www.nuigalway. ie/colleges-and-schools/arts-social-sciences-and-celtic-studies/staffprofiles/ lauramcloughlin/).

Anna Motzo is a lecturer in Italian at the School of Languages and Applied Linguistics at The Open University (UK). Her research focuses on innovative pedagogies in online language learning. Her current research interest is the use of social media in informal language learning practices.

Marina Orsini-Jones is Associate Head of School (International) and Course Director for the MA in English Language Teaching and Applied Linguistics in the School of Humanities at Coventry University (UK). Marina is a Principal Fellow and National Teaching Fellow of the Higher Education Academy and has been involved in CALL since 1985. She has contributed to over 100 conferences and has published work on action-research-led curricular innovation, threshold concepts in languages and linguistics, MOOCs, telecollaboration, and digital literacies. She is currently investigating how a 'blended MOOC' approach can support the reflection on language learning and teaching.

Anna Proudfoot is Head of Italian at the School of Languages and Applied Linguistics at The Open University (UK). Her research focuses on online language learning including student engagement in online learning activities.

Zaruhi Soghomonyan is a CELTA certified EL tutor. At present she teaches at French University in Armenia and is involved in QA procedures as an expert. Currently she is undertaking her DELTA course, with Module 1 already covered. She has TKT, CPE, BEC Higher certificates as well as C1 certificate of DELE. The scope of her professional interests and prior expertise includes teaching quality assurance, online instruction, e-moderating, lesson-planning, course development, and assessment.

Donatella Troncarelli is associate professor in Italian Linguistics and teaches 'Italian Grammar' and 'New Technologies for Language Teaching'. Presently she is the President of the post graduation course ELIIAS (E-learning for Italian language teaching) and Chair of the Bachelor degree course "Language and culture for teaching Italian as foreign language and for school". She has worked in the field of language course design and planning for both distance and on site education, and some of the projects she coordinated have been awarded with the European Language Labels.

Anne Van Marsenille is Belgian, she teaches Germanic languages at IHECS, a Higher Education Institution for Communication in Brussels, Belgium. She works for the international department and teaches abroad, mainly in Russian universities. Anne Van Marsenille holds a Doctorate in Education in the area of Foreign Language Learning - Informal Learning. In 2016 and in 2017, Anne Van Marsenille had courses in Intercultural and Organisational Communication at the Hofstede Centre. She is now an accredited lecturer in Intercultural and Organisational Management. She presents these topics to future business and communication specialists in Belgium, Russia and Asia.

Notes on contributors

Andrea Villarini is full professor of Modern Languages at the University for Foreigners of Siena. Currently Head of the Research Center for E-learning (FAST) and of the School of Specialisation in Teaching Italian as a Foreign Language, he supervised the planning and implementation of the first MOOC in Italy to teach Italian as an L2.

Jue Wang-Szilas holds a joint PhD in Language Science: Chinese Linguistics and Didactic from INALCO and in French as a Second Language from the University of Geneva. Since 2010, she has been working as lecturer and Research Associate in the Chinese Unit of the Department of East Asian Studies of the University of Geneva, where she coordinated the eTandem Chinese-French project involving three universities from Switzerland, France and China. Recently, she co-designed the first Introductory Chinese MOOC. Her current research interests include Computer-mediated Communication, Distance language training, and language MOOC design.

Zhang Wenxin[2] is a specialist in Chinese studies. Before founding her own educational consulting company in 2016, she worked at the University of Liverpool, Liverpool John Moores University, and the University of Chester as a senior lecturer in Mandarin Chinese. Dr Zhang's research interests include integrating new technologies into Mandarin learning, Mandarin teaching material development and psycholinguistics. At present, Dr Zhang is the director of Elite Technology and Education Limited. She is actively working with Mandarin learners from various backgrounds and conducting research to improve teaching practice.

Zhang Xinying[3] is lecturer in the School of Foreign Languages, Shenzhen University, China. She has been teaching English for non-English-major undergraduates since 2002. She has coordinated two provincial research projects on the topic of blended learning's application in EFL classrooms in China.

---

2. Zhang is the surname.

3. Zhang is the surname.

Her current research includes blended learning, MOOC design and language teaching.

Reviewers

Tita Beaven is a senior lecturer in Spanish at the School of Languages and Applied Linguistics at The Open University (UK). Her research is in the area of innovative pedagogy and technology in language learning and teaching and open education. She holds a Doctorate in Education (Educational Technology) from The Open University.

Anna Comas-Quinn is a senior lecturer at the School of Languages and Applied Linguistics at The Open University (UK). She led the development of LORO (http://loro.open.ac.uk), a repository of open educational resources for languages, was a Fellow of the Support Centre for Open Resources in Education (SCORE), and is a long-standing member of the organising committee of the UK-based OER conference. She has published on technology-enhanced and mobile language learning, teacher development and open educational resources and practices, and co-edited the first book on open practice in language teaching (https://doi.org/10.14705/rpnet.2013.9781908416100).

Chris Edwards is a lecturer in the Institute of Educational Technology at The Open University (UK). His teaching is in the Masters in Online and Distance Education, and in providing expertise to the Institution on levels and learning outcomes. He is a data wrangler, reporting on the effectiveness of the design of curriculum, and his research interests include learning analytics for improving curriculum and transitions, including to university study and enabling students to be more effective in their learning.

Regine Hampel is professor of Open and Distance Language Learning at The Open University (UK). As Associate Dean (Research Excellence) in the Faculty of Wellbeing, Education and Language Studies, she leads the unit's research portfolio. Her own research explores the impact of using new technologies for

Notes on contributors

language learning and teaching, focusing for example on the affordances of digital media, activity design, learner interaction and communication, online literacies, and teacher training. A recent project – 'Developing Online Teaching Skills' (DOTS) funded by the European Centre for Modern Languages – resulted in an edited book (Hampel & Stickler, 2015).

Mirjam Hauck is senior lecturer in the School of Languages and Applied Linguistics at The Open University (UK) and Senior Fellow of the UK's Higher Education Academy. She has recently returned from a secondment to the Centre for Collaborative Online International Learning (COIL) at the State University of New York, USA. She has written numerous articles and book chapters on the use of technologies for the learning and teaching of languages and cultures covering aspects such as task design, tutor role and training, and digital literacy. Apart from regular presentations at conferences, seminars and workshops in Europe and the USA, she serves on the EUROCALL executive committee. She is the Associate Editor of the CALL Journal and a member of the editorial board of ReCALL. More recently, her research and publications have centred on the impact of mediation and the relevance of digital literacy skills in the collaborative online (language) learning and teaching.

Agnes Kukulska-Hulme is professor of Learning Technology and Communication in the Institute of Educational Technology at The Open University (UK) and Past-President of the International Association for Mobile Learning. Her recent projects include the EU-funded MASELTOV project on personalised technologies for social inclusion, the British Council project on Mobile Pedagogy for English Language Teaching, and the OU/MK:Smart SALSA project on language learning in the next generation of smart cities. Her many publications include the co-edited book, Mobile Learning: The Next Generation (2016). She supervises doctoral students researching mobile and social learning with new technologies for communication and knowledge sharing.

Marie-Noelle Lamy is an emeritus professor with more than 20 years experience of distance learning and teaching at The Open University (UK). She has designed and implemented language courses for online study involving regular use of synchronous voice-enabled e-tutorials. She has researched extensively in the field of computer mediated communication for language learning, with a particular interest in real-time group conversations in multimodal settings. Current interests: methodologies for the description and analysis of online learning conversations, co-construction of group cultures by language learners in various online and social media environments, and cultural hegemonies in computer-assisted language learning.

Laura McLoughlin, PhD, is lecturer at the National University of Ireland, Galway, co-Director of the MA in Advanced Language Skills, Coordinator of the Diploma in Italian Online. Her research interests include Applied Linguistics, Audiovisual Translation, and CALL. She is the recipient of several international funding awards, and the winner of three European Language Labels. A list of recent publications can be found here.

Nathaniel Owen is a research associate at The Open University (UK). He has a PhD in language testing from the University of Leicester. He has published articles in peer-reviewed journals such as the International Journal of Research and Method in Education and book chapters in volumes such as The Routledge Handbook of English Language Teaching. He has experience of teaching English as a foreign language, with expertise in teaching EAP and exam preparation courses. He has previously worked as a Senior Research Manager at Cambridge Assessment. He is currently participating in funded research projects with ETS and the British Council.

Maria Luisa Pérez Cavana is lecturer in Languages at The Open University (UK). Her main research interests have been learner autonomy, learner centred pedagogy, and ePortfolios in relation to language learning. She was the OU leader researcher for the European project MAGICC (Modularising Multicultural and Multilingual Academic Communication Competences at BA and MA level) and she has been a member of the MOVEMe Project to develop a MOOC for Academic English for Erasmus Students. She is currently using phenomenology as a research method to study the lived experience of learning a language.

Notes on contributors

Fernando Rosell-Aguilar is senior lecturer in Spanish and Open Media Fellow at the School of Languages and Applied Linguistics at The Open University (UK). He is also a Senior Fellow of the Higher Education Academy. His research focuses on online language learning, mainly the use of apps, Twitter, and podcasting as teaching and learning tools. He has published his research in international journals such as Computers and Education, Language Learning and Technology, ReCALL, and CALL, and regularly presents at international conferences.

Ursula Stickler is senior lecturer in German in the School of Languages and Applied Linguistics at The Open University (UK). Her research focuses on independent and technology enhanced language learning and teacher training. She has published widely in the areas of Tandem learning, teacher training for online teaching, qualitative and mixed methods for Computer Assisted Language Learning (CALL) research, and eyetracking. She is also co-editor of System, the International Journal of Educational Technology and Applied Linguistics, and Senior Fellow of the Higher Education Academy, UK.

Tang Jinlan[4] is the deputy dean and professor of English in the School of Online and Continuing Education, Beijing Foreign Studies University, China. Her research has covered the areas of language assessment, tutor feedback, EFL teaching and learning in the e-learning environment. She has published over 30 research papers in academic journals, two books, and served as the principal investigator on a number of research projects. She is also the Secretary-General of the China Computer-Assisted Language Learning Association (2016–2020) (ChinaCALL, www.chinacall.org.cn).

---

4. Tang is the surname.

1 Introduction to *Beyond the language classroom: researching MOOCs and other innovations*

Kan Qian[1] and Stephen Bax[2]

The last ten years have witnessed an explosion in terms of the opportunities and resources available for language learning. A decade ago, the student of a new language was largely limited to print materials, recordings, the language classroom, or perhaps a visit abroad. Nowadays, he or she can sit in an armchair or at an airport, with a simple laptop computer or mobile phone, and access all the rich and varied input and the opportunities for interactive output which are key ingredients of the language learning process (cf. Lightbown & Spada, 2013). In addition, learners now have access to innumerable online resources to help them with grammar, vocabulary, pronunciation and more, and can even join free or cheap Massive Open Online Courses (MOOCs) to learn in social settings with help from educators and peers. In these spheres, language learning is at the same time becoming less formal – indeed the whole issue of informality in language learning is increasing in importance. As Lamy (2013) suggests in this quotation, the boundaries are becoming ever more blurred:

> "Formal learning can take place in a formal setting (e.g. instructor-anchored courses) or an informal one (e.g. Facebook adjuncts to courses). Informal learning too can occur in formal settings or informal ones" (p. 220).

In this sense, we see the rise of the truly 'liberated learner', freed from defined spaces and formal structures, eyes wide open at the sumptuous feast of language

---

1. The Open University, Milton Keynes, United Kingdom; qian.kan@open.ac.uk

2. The Open University, Milton Keynes, United Kingdom; stephen.bax@open.ac.uk

How to cite this chapter: Kan, Q., & Bax, S. (2017). Introduction to Beyond the language classroom: researching MOOCs and other innovations. In Q. Kan & S. Bax (Eds), *Beyond the language classroom: researching MOOCs and other innovations* (pp. 1-4). Research-publishing.net. https://doi.org/10.14705/rpnet.2017.mooc2016.666

Chapter 1

learning resources and opportunities spread out on offer, MOOCs and a whole lot more. It is easy to imagine such a learner asking, rightly or wrongly: who needs the classroom now?

This move out of the language classroom is not entirely new, of course. To take just one example, at the Open University in the United Kingdom, where the editors of this volume are based, we have been teaching language at a distance for over 25 years. Even so, every language teacher in the world must now be forced, by recent rapid increases in technological opportunities for language learning as exemplified by MOOCs and other innovations, to rethink all areas of their pedagogical activities.

It is this rapid change in the whole landscape of language education and its implications for pedagogy and practice which form the rationale and basis for this volume. Our aim is to work with our contributing authors to research and reflect on MOOCs and a number of other key innovations which we can hear calling loudly from outside the classroom walls. Our approach here is not to examine these innovations naively but to research them with caution and scepticism, in the light of the available evidence, in the awareness that not every innovation or new technology is necessarily an unalloyed benefit as it becomes normalised (Bax, 2003).

Our starting point is the MOVE-ME project funded by the European Union's Erasmus+ programme, the impetus for our cooperation, described by **Donatella Troncarelli and Andrea Villarini**. As they report there, the project aims at developing learning paths specifically for those many students in European 'mobility' programmes, and the use of MOOCs was considered potentially valuable in this endeavour, as they recount.

This is followed by six papers examining important and different aspects of a variety of MOOCs.

Zhang Xinying examines an innovative *MOOC +Flipped Classroom Mode* developed at Shenzhen University in China. **Inge de Waard and Kathy**

Demeulenaere research an interesting *MOOC-CLIL project* using MOOCs to increase language as well as social and online learning skills in a Belgian secondary school. **Jue Wang-Szilas and Joël Bellassen** then evaluate *The Introductory Chinese MOOC Kit*, the first Chinese MOOC for French speaking learners. Addressing some interesting questions about the aims of MOOCs in general, in the context of the EU-funded Move-Me project, **Laura McLoughlin and Francesca Magnoni** discuss and research *xMOOCs and cMOOCs*, and in the process consider how a MOOC can include metacognitive skills and strategies. An issue of increasing interest is how MOOCs fit with other educational activities. **Marina Orsini-Jones, Barbara Conde Gafaro, and Shooq Altamimi** examine through an interesting case study the ways in which a MOOC can be integrated with a formal curriculum. **Anna Motzo and Anna Proudfoot** close the section by discussing the experience of an innovative Italian MOOC offered by the Open University.

The following chapters then turn to examine other innovations.

Amanda Mason and Zhang Wenxin discuss mobile applications to support the learning of Chinese characters. The interesting and unusual example of a project in rural Armenia is examined by **Lilit Bekaryan, Zaruhi Soghomonyan, and Arusyak Harutyunyan**. On the subject of informal learning, **Tita Beaven, Mara Fuertes Gutiérrez, and Anna Motzo** consider and reflect on an innovative eTandem programme which had informality as a key ingredient. We end the volume with **Anne Van Marsenille**'s discussion of another informal approach, this time involving French-speaking higher education students in Brussels learning English and Dutch.

Together, then, these contributors offer a fascinating range of insights into the ways in which language learners, as we suggested above, are now emerging liberated from the classroom and other formal settings and finding for themselves new spaces, new directions and new resources. In the process, they are becoming more aware of their own learning strategies (partly due to the new learning design, and partly due to learners taking more control over their learning) as part of new modes of 'self-regulated learning' (Nussbaumer et al., 2015). Our contributors explore MOOCs as a salient example of these innovative language learning spaces, but they also address other important ways of learning beyond the classroom. They provide important research-based insights into how teachers and educational administrators should deal with these changes, to the benefit of the liberated learners and their teachers and guides of the future.

References

Bax, S. (2003). CALL—past, present and future. *System, 31*(1), 13-28. https://doi.org/10.1016/S0346-251X(02)00071-4

Lamy, M.-N. (2013). "We don't have to always post stuff to help us learn": informal learning through social networking in a beginners' Chinese group. In C. Meskill (Ed.), *Online teaching and learning: sociocultural perspectives* (pp. 219-238). London: Bloomsbury Academic.

Lightbown, P. M., & Spada, N. (2013). *How languages are learned* (4th ed.). Oxford: Oxford University Press.

Nussbaumer, A., Dahn, I., Kroop, S., Mikroyannidis, A., & Albert, D. (2015). Supporting self-regulated learning. In S. Kroop, A. Mikroyannidis, & M. Wolpers (Eds), *Responsive open learning environments : outcomes of research from the Role project* (pp. 17-48). Springer International Publishing. https://doi.org/10.1007/978-3-319-02399-1_2

2. Internationalization of higher education and the use of MOOCs to improve second language proficiency: the MOVE-ME project

Donatella Troncarelli[1] and Andrea Villarini[2]

Abstract

Over the last few decades the international dimension of higher education has grown significantly as internationalization has become a strategic goal for many governments. Students on the move worldwide reached five million in 2015 and their number is increasing at a rate of 10% each year. Many of these students need to develop proficiency in the language of the host country rapidly, in order to carry out their studies successfully and benefit from their experience abroad, on both personal and academic levels. Technology has the potential to accommodate these needs since it can enhance the process of learning offering flexible and self-paced paths, that can complement conventional language courses and extending ways of learning and teaching second languages. This paper presents the premises and the main choices of the MOVE-ME project – Massive Open Online Courses (MOOCs) for university students on the move in Europe –, funded under the Key Action 2 of the Erasmus+ program and based on the use of MOOCs to widen access to education resources for learning English and Italian for academic purposes.

Keywords: internationalization, language for academic purposes, informal language learning, MOOC.

---

1. University for Foreigners of Siena, Siena, Italy; troncarelli@unistrasi.it (author of the Introduction and Sections 1 and 2)

2. University for Foreigners of Siena, Siena, Italy; villarini@unistrasi.it (author of Section 3)

How to cite this chapter: Troncarelli, D., & Villarini, A. (2017). Internationalization of higher education and the use of MOOCs to improve second language proficiency: the MOVE-ME project . In Q. Kan & S. Bax (Eds), *Beyond the language classroom: researching MOOCs and other innovations* (pp. 5-14). Research-publishing.net. https://doi.org/10.14705/rpnet.2017.mooc2016.667

Chapter 2

1. Introduction

In recent decades, an increasingly integrated world economy has profoundly influenced higher education. In order to respond to the demand of a more globalised world, where goods and trade cross many borders, many governments have implemented policies and programs that have rapidly internationalized universities. As a result, millions of students go abroad to spend at least part of their studies in a foreign country. The number of students who choose to study outside of their home countries has doubled since 2000, reaching almost five million students in 2015, a figure estimated by the UNESCO Institute for Statistics (UIS, n.d.) to be three times larger than in 1990.

The increasing trend towards internationalization in Europe is also due in part to the efforts made by the European Commission to Internationalize higher education through the Bologna Process, which aims at harmonizing academic systems and at building a common European higher education area that can ensure compatible degree structures, transferable credits, and equal academic qualifications. Forty-eight countries inside and outside the EU have already implemented reforms in their higher education systems in order to foster intra-European student mobility, to increase employability and the attractiveness of higher education in Europe. Even though it is difficult to give precise figures of changing student mobility ascribable to the Bologna Process, because the criteria for measuring it have remained fairly weak and vary from country to country[3], it is believed that the overall increase in foreign students in Europe during the first 10 years of the Bologna Process was higher than 50% overall growth of the total number of foreign students in all countries of the world (Teichler, 2012; UIS, n.d.).

This growth does not include only European students but also students coming from other continents. The rate of students studying in Europe and coming from non EU countries especially from Asia, has increased in the last 20 years.

---

3. The way European countries consider foreign students is heterogeneous. Some countries even include in their mobile or international student statistics students who have moved to the country before starting their university studies, while other countries count mobile students among home students during their experience in another country (Teichler, 2012).

China, India and Korea encourage students to study abroad and, at present, Asian students account for 53% of all students studying abroad worldwide (Piro, 2016). Also, the number of students coming from Africa is increasing and the demand for studying abroad is predicted to mirror general population growth.

Though the most common destination countries for mobile students are the USA, UK, Australia, France, Germany, Russia, Japan and Canada (OECD, 2016; UIS, n.d.), even countries that were less affected by steady international trends in the past, such as Ireland and Italy, are now strongly involved in the internationalization process, according to UIS. The number of international students in Ireland has risen to 8.8% of the overall student body in the academic year 2015-16, with an increase of more than 25 percent in the last 3 years. In Italy, international students were 3.9% of the overall student body in the academic year 2015-16, a figure far below the European average that reaches 8.6% (European Migration Network, 2014). The majority of mobile students in Italy come from European, Asian and African countries, such as Albania, Romania, Greece, China, Cameroon and Morocco. Except for Chinese students, for the students coming from these countries, Italy represents the preferred destination for studies within the EU (European Migration Network, 2014).

2. Internationalization in Italy

Many countries have participated in international educational activities for a long time, attracting students from abroad and providing international and cross-cultural perspectives. Italy has been one of these as it has been attracting students from North Europe since the Renaissance. The flows of students coming to Italy to study art and literature have been continuous but not considerable (De Mauro, 2002; Diadori, Palermo, & Troncarelli, 2015). Recently, this form of traditional internationalization has been strengthened by other forms of student mobility.

First of all, the Erasmus+ Project, responsible for the mobility of 250,000 in Europe, according to the European Commission data, has brought to Italy more than 20,000 students per year and has allowed 25,000 Italian students to experience studying abroad in the academic year 2015-16. Besides being one of the top European senders and receivers of Erasmus students, Italy has also started to promote programs for the recruitment of foreign students in the last decade.

In 2006, the program 'Invest Your Talent in Italy' was launched with the aim of attracting postgraduate students from countries of trade interest for Italy, such as Colombia, South Africa, India, Turkey and Brazil. Two years before, the Marco Polo program had been launched to promote studying in Italy among Chinese students. The program is an agreement between Italian and Chinese governments that facilitates enrolment in Italian Universities and in obtaining a student visa. To promote further studying in Italy among Chinese young people, the Turandot program was launched in 2009. The program focuses on arts, music, and design, allowing students to enrol in Italian Institutes of High Training in Art and Music. Therefore, the number of Chinese students in the Italian higher education system has increased by 222% in five years since 2009, thanks to both programs[4].

The growth of international students in Italy is also related to the promotion of joint programs and double degrees with overseas universities. Recently, this has become a successful activity in increasing internationalization in Italy.

3. International students' language needs

Language plays an important role for international students in choosing their destination country. It is not an accident that English language countries such as the USA, UK, Australia and Canada are among the top destinations (UIS, n.d.). Italy, because of its long tradition as a destination for students coming from North Europe to study literature and arts, as mentioned above, offers a limited choice of degree courses in English. In the majority of the courses, Italian is the medium of instruction. This language policy choice, in line with the plurilingual approach of the Council of Europe that safeguards linguistic diversity, can

---

4. The source of these data is Uni-Italia, an association for international education supported by the Italian Ministry of Education and the Ministry for Foreign Affairs: http://www.uni-italia.it/it/

represent either a means of attraction or an obstacle. Many students choose to come to Italy because of its language and culture. Nevertheless, the language proficiency level required is not adequate to cope with studying in Italy[5].

As the Common European Framework of Reference (CEFR) (Council of Europe, 2001) points out, language proficiency has not only a vertical dimension described by the communicative level achieved, but also a horizontal dimension related to parameters of the tasks and communicative activities that take place in the domain in which the use of the language is involved. In other words, a language certification level B1 or B2 certifies the student as an independent and confident user of the language in many common everyday situations, but it does not guarantee that the student can master the language needed for studying in a foreign language.

Consequently, international students should be supported in developing language and academic skills for successful university studies across disciplines. However, at present, the courses open to international and Erasmus students in Italy are designed to develop only some of those skills because they are more oriented to develop the vertical dimension of the communicative competence, rather than enlarging knowledge and skills related to the specific tasks students are required to accomplish in the educational domain and within a particular field of knowledge. Thus, most of the time students have to endure by themselves the burden of mastering linguistic structures, lexicon, and discourse structures in order to understand lectures and texts, as well as learning how to express their ideas in the most appropriate style for their purpose and audience.

Moreover, students need to consolidate, extend and develop their proficiency in academic Italian in a short time, without leaving aside the curriculum subjects. Courses based on intensive tuition or weekly classes are not effective because students have little time to dedicate to language learning and their attendance

---

[5]. Chinese students are required to achieve CEFR B1 for studying at degree level or above. Language requirements are less demanding for them than those for other international students who have to demonstrate having a B2 level of language proficiency to enrol for a Bachelor's or Master's degree. Erasmus students can experience studying in Italy even with a language proficiency under the B1 level.

becomes very irregular. Therefore, new learning solutions have to be found out and technologies can be the key for new opportunities and self-paced learning.

4. Teaching language using MOOCs: the MOVE-ME project

One of the new learning solutions is to provide courses in the form of MOOCs, which allow very large numbers of learners to study at any time and in any place free of charge. Furthermore, a language MOOC enables students in international mobility to increase their proficiency in the language used to deliver the university courses they are going to attend, even before they leave at no extra cost.

However, as known, MOOCs are usually courses with very large numbers of enrolled students, numbers that are generally considered not suitable for language training. Consequently, the risk could be to provide a course without any chance of success (because it would be attended simultaneously by too large a number of students). In other words, it is to take on a new difficult challenge; namely the one about creating a course that can be successfully attended by hundreds of students, and at the same time can actually provide language training for academic purposes.

To take on the above challenge and with the landscape outlined in previous sections, the MOVE-ME project has been devised. The project aims at creating two MOOCs teaching English and Italian for academic purposes, designed for students who want to study in Italian and English universities. This project is founded by the Erasmus+ program Key Action 2 – Cooperation for innovation and the exchange of good practices – and it involves six partners:

- University for Foreigners of Siena, Italy;

- University of Galway, Ireland;

- The Open University, UK;

- Federazione Nazionale Insegnanti, Italy;

- Computer Technology Institute and Press 'Diophantus', Greece;

- Institutul de Științe ale Educației, Romania.

This project is led by the University for Foreigners of Siena that has in recent years gained a rich experience in the field of language training and the use of new technologies. It is one of the two public Italian universities specializing in the teaching of Italian as a second language. In the last ten years, the University for Foreigners of Siena has worked out several projects based on the use of technologies to meet specific learning needs and to experience new pedagogical solutions for distance language learning, some of which were rewarded with the European Language Label[6]. Among the last experiences, there is the first MOOC for learning Italian created by an Italian institution named 'Introduction to Italian', an open course for beginners, hosted by FutureLearn (www.futurelearn.com/courses/learn-italian), which involved more than 48,000 learners in its first run.

The interest of the University for Foreigners of Siena in developing language courses for academic purposes, originates not only from the inclusion of these types of training in its educational syllabus, but also from the strong demand of academic Italian, both in general and within this institution. The internationalization rate at University for Foreigners of Siena reached 13% in the academic year 2015-16, a figure far beyond the national and European rates (UNISTRASI data[7]). Therefore, to support students in developing skills in academic Italian is a crucial matter for successful study at university and for increasing internationalization. Moreover, the University for Foreigners of Siena, as far as Italian language learning is concerned, caters to the needs of other universities in the same area and in other Italian regions.

---

6. The European Language Label is an award of the European Commission given annually to innovative language learning projects involving new techniques in language teaching and spreading the knowledge of languages' existence, thereby promoting good practice: http://ec.europa.eu/education/initiatives/language-label_en

7. http://www.unistrasi.it/1/558/2752/Area_dati.htm

Thus, the MOVE-ME project was devised to meet this demand and to give an appropriate answer to the specific learning needs of students on the move. Therefore, it aims at developing learning paths specifically for students in European 'mobility' programs and intends to develop language fluency for communication in academic contexts. The learning paths will be implemented as a MOOC on the FutureLearn platform, in order to make them accessible to the largest number of students on the move. Learning materials are designed for self-study and will be produced in two languages, English and Italian. As mentioned on Kan's profile[8], the two MOOCs will support learners in the acquisition of competences and skills necessary for understanding and producing oral and written expository texts relating to specific disciplines. In particular, the project aims to:

- increase students' awareness of the language learning process and knowing how to use effective learning strategies;

- increase students' understanding of written and oral expository texts relating to academic disciplines;

- improve the quality of oral and written expository texts produced by students and relating to academic disciplines;

- improve students' performance at oral and written exams in L2;

- support students in learning to learn;

- provide guidelines and a syllabus for the creation of MOOCs for languages for academic purposes;

- provide specific guidelines for the evaluation of language MOOCs;

---

8. http://wels.open.ac.uk/people/qk8?

- create Open Educational Resources (OERs) which support autonomous and independent learning;

- develop a website hosting all OERs created during the project.

The choice to develop the learning materials in English and Italian is due to the availability of a wide literature on academic English that allows the project team to have a theoretical framework for rethinking learning paths from the perspective of open online learning. The rich literature on academic English also offers many cues for teaching a less wide spread second language such as Italian.

The two MOOCs for both languages include six modules that will last six weeks. The first one outlines the main features of academic discourse and texts and raises awareness about learning how to learn a second language for academic purposes. The second one deals with reading comprehension, while the third one focuses on listening comprehension. The following ones are dedicated to production and will guide students to write an essay, and to prepare and deliver an oral presentation.

Together with the MOOCs, as mentioned in the list of the project's aims above, the MOVE-ME project will create a repository of open educational resources to be used by teachers and learners, that will be hosted on the project's website (www.movemeproject.eu). Teachers can use it to develop their own second language teaching paths, and learners can use it to improve specific aspects of their competence in English or in Italian for academic purposes.

5. Conclusion

The choice to use a MOOC to support students' mobility is linked to the flexibility of this educational pattern (Bárcena & Martín-Monje, 2014). MOOCs, as online courses, can be followed by students who are going to leave their country to study abroad or by students already studying in another country. Moreover, MOOCs are free courses that can be used by those who cannot afford to attend face-to-face courses. Another reason that encouraged delivering the courses on a MOOC platform was the interest in verifying the effectiveness of its methodology with this profile of students.

Even though the advantages of using MOOCs for teaching a second language for academic purposes to university students are many, a couple of questions still require an answer. The first one is related with the effectiveness of MOOCs as a means to teach a second language, and the second one is the possibility and the opportunity of using MOOC technology and methodology for curricular activities. The MOVE-ME project aims to address these questions directly.

References

Bárcena, E., & Martín-Monje E. (Eds). (2014). *Language MOOCs: providing learning, transcending boundaries.* De Gruyter Open.
Council of Europe. (2001). *Common European framework of reference for languages: learning teaching assessment.* Cambridge: Cambridge University Press.
De Mauro, T. (2002). *Italiano 2000: i pubblici e le motivazioni dell'italiano diffuso fra stranieri.* Roma: Bulzoni.
Diadori, P., Palermo, M., & Troncarelli, D. (2015). *Insegnare l'italiano come seconda lingua.* Roma: Carocci.
European Migration Network. (2014). *Immigration of international students to Italy.* Roma. Edizioni IDOS. http://ec.europa.eu/dgs/home-affairs/what-we-do/networks/european_migration_network/reports/docs/emn-studies/immigration-students/14a._italy_national_report_international_students_april2013_final_en.pdf
OECD. (2016). *Education at a glance 2016: OECD Indicators.* Paris: OECD Publishing.
Piro, J. M. (2016). *Revolutionizing global higher education policy: innovation and the Bologna process.* New York: Routledge.
Teichler, U. (2012). International student mobility and the Bologna process. *Research in Comparative and International Education,* 7(1), 34-49. https://doi.org/10.2304/rcie.2012.7.1.34
UIS. (n.d.). *UNESCO institute for statistics.* http://data.uis.unesco.org/

3 Researching into a MOOC embedded flipped classroom model for college English Reading and Writing course

Zhang Xinying[1]

Abstract

There is obvious pressure for higher education institutions to undergo transformation now in China. Reflecting this, the computer and information technology give rise to the development of a Massive Open Online Course (MOOC) embedded flipped classroom. Flipped classroom approaches replace the traditional transmissive teaching with engaging in-class and pre-/post-class work. This paper provides an overview of relevant literature about the emergence of the flipped classroom and its links to pedagogy and educational outcomes, followed by an analysis of the survey results of a one year experiment using a flipped classroom approach which involved 800 students at Shenzhen University. The questionnaire completed by 230 students at the end of the second semester investigated students' attitudes as well as their perceived benefits and effects of this new approach. The results reveal that the majority of students preferred the flipped method, and over 50% of them felt they were making good progress in many aspects of their English language learning. The paper argues that a MOOC embedded flipped approach promotes student active, autonomous, and collaborative learning skills, and it contributes to a better understanding of technology-enhanced, student-centred learning environments.

Keywords: MOOCs, flipped classroom, active learning, college English course, China.

---

1. Shenzhen University, Shenzhen, China; zhangxinying@szu.edu.cn

How to cite this chapter: Zhang, X. (2017). Researching into a MOOC embedded flipped classroom model for college English Reading and Writing course. In Q. Kan & S. Bax (Eds), *Beyond the language classroom: researching MOOCs and other innovations* (pp. 15-27). Research-publishing.net. https://doi.org/10.14705/rpnet.2017.mooc2016.668

Chapter 3

1. Introduction

College English, a compulsory course in all higher education curriculum in China, is undergoing reforms in both content and teaching pedagogy. College English curriculum requirements, commissioned by The Ministry for Higher Education (2007), advocate "a computer-assisted and classroom-based teaching model" (p. 8). Wang and Wang (2011) point out that computer and information technology can assist student-centred and teacher-facilitated teaching models at the tertiary level.

While MOOCs have become a focus in the Chinese education field for their merits as 'open', 'online', and 'massive', blended learning offers potential solutions to the problems experienced in MOOCs, e.g. a high drop-out rate. By 'blended learning', I use the definition of the North American Council for Online Learning as reported in Camahalan and Ruley (2014),

> "a learning approach that combined the best elements of online and face-to-face learning (NACOL, 2013). [...] According to the North American Council for Online Learning (NACOL, 2013), blended learning is likely to emerge as the predominant model of the future, and [will] become far more common than face-to-face or online learning alone" (pp. 2-3).

Flipped classroom approaches are one type of blended learning. As claimed by Abeysekera and Dawson (2014), in a flipped classroom, "the information transmission component of a traditional face-to-face lecture [...] is moved out of class time" (p. 2) and presented to learners outside class, for example in the form of a MOOC. Class time is replaced with active and collaborative tasks and personalised teaching.

In the academic year 2014-2015, the Shenzhen University adopted the flipped method in the college English Reading and Writing course. Part of teaching materials was put into a MOOC, using the nine flipped classroom design principles proposed by Kim, Kim, Khera, and Getman (2014), further discussed below. A group of 800 students was required to complete the MOOC learning prior to their weekly two hour face-to-face English classes.

In China, traditional teacher-centred language teaching models prevail in education at secondary school level. So when students start undergraduate courses, they need to adjust to the student-centred new approach. This study aims to investigate students' attitudes as well as their experience of the flipped classroom approach, which was totally new to them. The findings will help designers and educators better understand technology-enhanced and student-centred learning environments so as to improve student learning experiences.

2. Literature review

According to Andrews, Leonard, Colgrove, and Kalinowski (2011), active learning is the kind of learning that happens when "an instructor stops lecturing and students work on a question or task designed to help them understand a concept" (p. 394). The characteristics associated with active learning are conscientiousness, concentration, and a deep approach to learning, which has a positive impact on student achievements (Richardson, Abraham, & Bond, 2012). The flipped classroom approach creates the environment which makes it possible to let students engage in active learning (Berrett, 2012; Milman, 2012; Strayer, 2012). This active learning is encouraged by a range of interactive activities, which are originally the information-transmission component of a traditional lecture (Abeysekera & Dawson, 2014). Abeysekera and Dawson (2014) outline the following set of pedagogical approaches for the flipped classroom:

- move most information-transmission teaching out of class;

- use class time for learning activities that are active and social;

- require students to complete pre- and/or post-class activities to fully benefit from in-class work.

Chapter 3

As mentioned by Kim et al. (2014),

> "[f]lipped classroom models have attempted to address these challenges by allocating more class time for active learning and by leveraging accessibility to advanced technologies to support a blended learning approach. [...] Teachers in turn are able to commit more in-class time to monitoring student performance and providing adaptive and instant feedback to an individual or groups of students (Fulton, 2012; Herreid & Schiller, 2013; Hughes, 2012)" (p. 37-50).

English learning is the process of constant practicing and outputting, instead of listening to lectures and mere inputting (He, 2003).

The following nine design principles for the flipped classroom proposed by Kim et al. (2014, pp. 43-46) guided the design of the English Reading and Writing flipped classroom:

- provide an opportunity for students to gain first exposure prior to class;
- provide an incentive for students to prepare for class;
- provide a mechanism to assess student understanding;
- provide clear connections between in-class and out-of-class activities;
- provide clearly defined and well-structured guidance;
- provide enough time for students to carry out the assignments;
- provide facilitation for building a learning community;
- provide prompt/adaptive feedback on individual or group works;
- provide familiar technologies easy to access.

O'Flaherty and Phillips (2015) searched eight academic literature databases and internet resources worldwide, and found 28 empirical study papers looking at flipped classroom approaches in higher education. Excluding four papers which did not discuss the outcomes of a flipped classroom approach, 24 studies all suggested the positive impact of this model. Bishop and Verleger (2013) reviewed 24 studies on the flipped classroom approach and had the same conclusion.

Our college English Reading and Writing course used such an approach which provided students with access to MOOC lectures prior to in-class sessions, so that students were prepared to better participate in interactive and further activities in class, such as problem-solving, discussions, presentations and debates. This study aims to investigate if such an approach is appropriate for the Chinese context, in particular to answer the following research questions:

- What are students' attitudes towards a MOOC and flipped classroom approach?

- What are the perceived benefits in terms of their English proficiency and study skills?

3. Research methods

This study was carried out in the 2014-15 academic year, involving 800 students (non-English majors) of the college English Reading and Writing course in 23 classes. The average class size was around 35 students. This was a compulsory course with eight to 12 credits. An English placement test divided all freshmen (approx. 7,000 students) into three levels at the beginning of the academic year. The top 10% of the freshmen, who were called 'Level-A' students, were required to use a MOOC flipped classroom approach for this course.

Eleven units of teaching materials from the English Reading and Writing textbook were produced into a MOOC (Figure 1) on the University Open

Online platform (https://mooc1.chaoxing.com/course/80447257.html)[2]. This platform can record students' performances, video-watching completion rate, visit frequency, and task completion rate. The MOOC covered key vocabulary, reading comprehension, text analysis and writing skills. 150 minutes of video of each unit ranging from formal teaching to activities with video clips for students to complete every two weeks. Level-A students were required to complete self-paced MOOC learning before class, followed by two hour, face-to-face, in-class learning every week. The face-to-face sessions were devoted to interactive and collaborative activities: peer interaction activities (group discussion or group project), and teacher-student interaction activities (presentation with feedback, project with feedback, debate with feedback or writing with feedback). Acting as facilitators instead of instructors, teachers' main roles were checking understanding, facilitating learning, and further exploring the theme of each unit. The teaching experiment lasted for 32 weeks, i.e. two semesters.

Figure 1. Screenshot of the MOOC for the college English Reading and Writing course

---

2. A MOOC platform in China hosted by Shenzhen University.

To investigate students' perception of the approach and the perceived benefits in terms of their English proficiency and study skills, 230 Level-A students (33% male and 67% female) were randomly invited to complete an online questionnaire in a computer lab. The questionnaire[3] consisted of three parts: overall attitudes on flipped classroom model; self-evaluation of the impact on their learning; and overall satisfaction with this learning approach as well as the study time outside the classroom each week. Both multiple-choice and open-ended questions were designed. The questionnaire was in Chinese to avoid misunderstanding.

4. Results

The results reveal that the majority of students preferred flipped methods compared with traditional teaching approaches, and although there was no proficiency test to prove their progress, a high percentage of students felt that their English reading and writing skills had been improved. Below are the key findings from the survey.

4.1. MOOC and flipped classroom model, collaborative and peer learning style

Table 1 below gives a summary of respondents' attitudes towards (1) the MOOC and flipped classroom model, (2) collaborative learning style, and (3) peer learning style.

Table 1. Attitudes to the new model, and collaborative and peer learning style

	Strongly agree	Agree	Not sure	Slightly disagree	Disagree
I like this MOOC and flipped classroom learning model.	16.1%	40.9%	33.5%	5.2%	3.9%
I like this collaborative learning style.	16.1%	59.6%	15.9%	6.5%	1.4%
I like peer learning.	10.4%	48.7%	25.7%	9.6%	5.2%

---

3. Available from https://research-publishing.box.com/s/fx4wy2zr61ep0f5cblvqb9yzjqxcy9v3

On average, combining those who agree and strongly agree, 57% of the respondents were positive towards the MOOC flipped classroom model, while 9% did not accept this change. Over a third of respondents (33.5%) were not sure. The positive attitude was supported by comments in the open section:

> "This is fashionable and encourages us to do more autonomous learning and independent thinking" (Student A).
>
> "This new model helps us explore in language learning and the best thing is I can set my own pace to study and allocate time accordingly" (Student B).

As lecturing on vocabulary or language points in class has been replaced by MOOC, teachers' responsibilities were shifted to more personalised tutoring that suited the needs of each student. Students responded in the questionnaire by saying:

> "My teacher gave me feedback each time I did my oral project or writing assignments. I feel closer to my teacher, compared with the other teachers lecturing mainly in the class" (Student C).

Teamwork was popular in this MOOC flipped classroom teaching model. Students were divided into groups (usually four students to one group) to do their oral projects or research projects. 76% of respondents liked collaborative work, whilst only 8% gave negative evaluation. 16% of them were not sure.

Almost 60% of respondents favoured peer learning and agreed that they learnt from each other, but 15% of them held the opposite view. Around 25% of respondents were uncertain. There was further evidence from the open questions that support the positive attitude:

> "I like my teammates in a particular way and for sure we will stay in the same team in the possible future opportunities. I never realised that I can learn so much from my classmates" (Student D).

Of those who felt negative about it, one student said in the open question:

> "I am not used to this new stuff and I haven't seen anything beneficial" (Student E).

It is not surprising that some respondents were negative or unsure about the new module. As explained earlier, secondary education in China is predominantly teacher-centred, so when students first enter university, they find it hard to adjust to the new teaching style in which they have to take control of their studies.

4.2. Perceived progress

On average, 51% of the respondents felt that they had made progress in English reading and writing, as evidenced in the open comments:

> "I have my vocabulary size enlarged and I know more about how to use them and I have learned how to use different sentence structures and phrases" (Student F).

> "I have acquired knowledge from the MOOC lecturing and have learned to use them in my writing and speaking. I have more sophisticated words to choose from when I am writing" (Student G).

It is worth noting is that a high proportion of respondents were uncertain if they had made any progress. This might be due to the following reasons: (1) they had never been asked these types of questions so they were unable to make a judgement or evaluate their own progress, and (2) they evaluated their progress in terms of their tests and exam results rather than their communicative competence.

4.3. Overall satisfaction

59% of respondents were satisfied with this MOOC and flipped classroom learning model, with 12% unsatisfied, and the remaining unsure.

4.4. Time spent on learning outside the classroom

When asked how many hours on average were spent on English study after class, 14.4% of respondents spent more than ten hours per week, and 58.7% students spent between five to ten hours per week. This percentage is significantly higher than Level-B students who did not take part in this experiment, among which 33% of students spent 1-2 hours per week, 25% spent two to three hours, and 19% spent three to four hours.

5. Discussion

The above findings suggest that a MOOC flipped classroom model is an effective combination of internet technology and face-to-face teaching for teaching college English. This approach appears to offer two clear benefits: students appear to be more motivated and engaging; and they spend more time learning outside their class hours. This supports Richardson et al.'s (2012) definition of active learning, when learners take initiative and become more conscientious, which has a positive impact on the classroom learning, as teachers also noticed more interactions in the classroom.

Freed from traditional language classrooms, students have realised that language learning needs constant practicing, interaction, and personalised feedback from teachers. Students benefit from having more time after class to spend on areas that need strengthening. The high satisfaction rate (59%) with the new teaching model indicates that the combination of MOOC with interactive activities using the designing principles as proposed by Abeysekera and Dawson (2014) worked in this study. This does not mean that there is no room for improvement. On the contrary, as 41% were either not satisfied or unsure, there is huge room for improvement.

We also need to bear in mind that university students' motivation for learning English is largely instrumental. In China, all employers require the result of the College English Test (CET), which is a language proficiency test taken by university students after graduation. As the MOOC flipped classroom model is not designed for passing the exam, students might resist the innovation. We need to raise student awareness that high exam scores do not necessarily equal language competence by creating authentic communication opportunities.

In short, the findings from this study suggest that this new approach, favoured by the majority of students in previous studies (Bishop & Verleger, 2013; O'Flaherty & Phillips, 2015), can be successfully implemented in the Chinese educational context. Students will need more guidance, such as an induction programme, to teach them autonomous and online learning skills before putting them on the courses that use flipped classroom approaches.

6. Conclusion

This study researches into the MOOC flipped classroom model piloted across Level-A students taking the college English Reading and Writing course at Shenzhen University. The study found that 57% of respondents surveyed liked to learn from the MOOC outside the classroom before meeting the teacher in the class to engage in interactive language activities. 59% surveyed were satisfied with the course delivered using this model, with 51% feeling they had made progress with their English reading and writing.

The paper argues that the flipped classroom approach is applicable to the Chinese higher education context, and that it can help to improve active, autonomous, and collaborative learning skills. The paper hopes to contribute to a better understanding of technology-enhanced and student-centred learning environments.

The limitation of this study is that it primarily relied upon the participants' perceptions of their own experiences in the flipped classroom to evaluate the quality of the teaching model. Further research is needed to link students' perceived benefits with attainment so as to establish the effectiveness of the flipped classroom approach.

The current study is based on the class size of 35 students approximately. Future research can explore if this MOOC embedded flipped classroom teaching model is applicable to large English as a foreign language classrooms in China.

References

Abeysekera, L., & Dawson, P. (2014). Motivation and cognition load in the flipped classroom: definition, rational and a call for research. *Higher Education Research & Development, 34*(1), 1-14. https://doi.org/10.1080/07294360.2014.934336

Andrews, T. M., Leonard, M. J., Colgrove, C. A., & Kalinowski S. T. (2011). Active learning not associated with student learning in a random sample of college biology courses. *Life Sciences Education, 10*(4), 394-405. https://doi.org/10.1187/cbe.11-07-0061

Berrett, D. (2012). How 'flipping' the classroom can improve the traditional lecture. *The Chronicle of Higher Education.* http://chronical. Com/article/How-Flipping-the-Classroom/130857/

Bishop, J. L., &Verleger, A. (2013). *The flipped classroom: a survey of the research.* http://www.asee.org/public/conferences/20/papers/6219/view

Camahalan, F. M. G., & Ruley, A. G. (2014). Blended learning and teaching writing: a teacher action research project. *Journal of Instructional Pedagogies, 15*(October), 1-13. http://www.aabri.com/manuscripts/142043.pdf?

Fulton, K. (2012). Upside down and inside out: flip your classroom to improve student learning. *Learning & Leading with Technology, 39*(8), 12-17.

He, Z. R. (2003). Foreign Language is to be learned by practicing. *Journal of Foreign Languages, 2*, 51-56.

Herreid, C., & Schiller, N. (2013). Case studies and the flipped classroom. *Journal of College Science Teaching, 42*(5), 62.

Hughes, H. (2012). Introduction to flipping the college classroom. In T. Amiel & B. Wilson (Eds), *Proceedings from world conference on educational multimedia, hypermedia and telecommunications 2012* (pp. 2434-2438). Chesapeake: AACE.

Kim, M. K., Kim, S. M., Khera, O, & Getman, J. (2014). The experience of three flipped classrooms in an urban university: an exploration of design principles. *The Internet and Higher Education, 22*(July), 37-50. https://doi.org/10.1016/j.iheduc.2014.04.003

Milman, N. (2012). The flipped classroom strategy: what is it and how can it best be used. *Distance Learning, 9*(3), 85-87.

NACOL. (2013). North American Council for Online Learning. http://www.inacol.org

O'Flaherty, J., & Phillips, C. (2015). The use of flipped classrooms in higher education: a scoping review. *The Internet and Higher Education, 25*, 85-95. https://doi.org/10.1016/j.iheduc.2015.02.002

Richardson, M., Abraham, C., & Bond, R. (2012). Psychological correlates of university students' academic performance: a systematic review and meta-analysis. *Psychological Bulletin, 138*(2), 353-387. https://doi.org/10.1037/a0026838

Strayer, J. F. (2012). How learning in an inverted classroom influenced cooperation, innovation and task orientation. *Learning Environments Research, 15*(2), 171-193. https://doi.org/10.1007/s10984-012-9108-4

The Ministry for Higher Education. (2007). *College English curriculum requirements*. Beijing, China: Foreign Language Teaching and Research Press.

Wang, S. R., & Wang, H. X. (2011). Analysis for social needs for college English. *Foreign Languages in China, 9*, 4-11.

4 The MOOC-CLIL project: using MOOCs to increase language, and social and online learning skills for 5th grade K-12 students

Inge de Waard[1] and Kathy Demeulenaere[2]

Abstract

This study comprises the outcomes and methods of a one year project using Content and Language Integrated Learning (CLIL) and Massive Open Online Courses (MOOCs) embedded in K-12 classes. The Self-Regulated Learning (SRL) of 42 students enrolled in three 5th grade classes were monitored. The students took the MOOC-CLIL class for one year (2015-2016) at the Guldensporencollege (GUSCO), a Belgian secondary school in Kortrijk. In this weekly, two-hour class, the 16-17 year old students were increasingly guided towards autonomously choosing and learning from MOOCs in a non-native language. At the last phase of the project, the students were asked to autonomously choose and engage in a MOOC. The study used a three step approach to increase autonomous, online learning. Students could choose from French and English MOOCs, while their mother tongue is Flemish (Belgian Dutch). The project consisted of a practical teaching/learning approach rolled out by the teachers, and a research approach enabling a step-by-step evaluation of self-regulated learning. Findings include an increase of practical language use, confidence in planning autonomous learning, and increased social learning skills.

Keywords: K12, MOOC, lifelong learning, social learning, language learning skills.

1. The Open University, Milton Keynes, United Kingdom; ingedewaard@gmail.com

2. Guldensporencollege, Kortrijk, Belgium; kathy.demeulenaere@gusco.be

How to cite this chapter: De Waard, I., & Demeulenaere, K. (2017). The MOOC-CLIL project: using MOOCs to increase language, and social and online learning skills for 5th grade K-12 students . In Q. Kan & S. Bax (Eds), *Beyond the language classroom: researching MOOCs and other innovations* (pp. 29-42). Research-publishing.net. https://doi.org/10.14705/rpnet.2017.mooc2016.669

Chapter 4

1. Introduction

The aim of this research was two-fold: exploring the use of MOOCs to increase online learning skills in K-12 students through a scaffolded approach; and to provide an open, authentic language opportunity within a school setting. MOOC use has been studied in various contexts but – to the knowledge of the authors – it has never been used in a CLIL set-up, nor have K-12 students been given the opportunity to autonomously choose which MOOC they could take in a secondary school setting.

MOOCs were used within class options offering CLIL, which is an approach for learning content through an additional language. It is based on methodological principles established by research combining language immersion and content-based instruction (Marsh, 2002). In the past, CLIL has proven to "increase vocabularies of technical and semi-technical terms and of general academic language because of the subjects they have studied" (Scott & Beade, 2014, p. 8), as well as provide effective opportunities of using new language skills. Although the project was situated within a formal school setting – at GUSCO in Kortrijk, Belgium – the MOOC-CLIL classes were set up so that the teachers scaffolded the students towards autonomous learning. This MOOC-CLIL pilot answers a call by Grover, Pea, and Cooper (2014) who suggest developing more MOOC based pilot projects.

2. Literature

MOOCs have been used in various ways, including the flipped classroom approach. According to Bishop and Verleger (2013), "[t]he flipped classroom is a pedagogical method, which employs asynchronous video lectures and practice problems, such as homework, and active, group-based problem solving activities in the classroom" (p. 1). This pedagogical approach complements traditional classroom teaching through integration of a whole or particular parts of a course in K-12 or higher education (Najafi, Evans, & Federico, 2014; de Waard, 2015). At GUSCO, MOOC content has been integrated into existing courses in a blended format since 2013. The blending of MOOCs within formal school settings was proposed by Bruff, Fisher, McEwen, and Smith (2013) as a sound way to widen MOOC use. Liu and Cavanaugh (2012) investigated blended introductory mathematics courses and they concluded that having a teacher present in a blended learning setting positively affects student outcomes. As students only had two mandatory hours per week for following MOOCs, we needed to consider the impact of only partially participating in MOOCs. However, research has showed that those learners who access only portions of a course's content still have meaningful learning experiences (de Waard, Kukulska-Hulme, & Sharples, 2015; Ho et al., 2015).

2.1. Learning from a variety of MOOCs and designs

As stated by de Waard et al. (2011), "[t]here is [...] a need to determine design principles for MOOCs to effectively maximise their self-organising, self-referencing, and knowledge-producing capabilities" (p. 112). This element of understanding is especially needed when considering the variety of current MOOC platforms, as "there is a clear difference in pedagogical approach [... and] design of the user interface, [...] which results in a challenge to understand all the options within different MOOC platforms" (de Waard, 2015, n.p.). The variety of MOOC designs in combination with the reality of learning to learn in and from MOOCs increased the need for a blended approach so students would be introduced to MOOCs in a teacher supported setting.

2.2. CLIL and teacher role when including online resources and interactions

By opening up the classroom setting to include content and interactions from online resources – in this case MOOCs – an additional CLIL learning environment is created. However, young learners have less formal educational experience and may require very different supports than older, more educated learners (Guzdial, 2014). This points again towards using a scaffolded approach to increase CLIL success. In her book on telecollaborative language learning for CLIL, Dooly (2008) proposed that the teacher could take up the role of a guide to support the learners online, as well as in the blended classroom setting. Pellegrino, de Santo, and Vitale (2013) also emphasise the importance of scaffolded teacher support to show the students how to proceed before engaging in online interactions with peers, to ensure a meaningful, communicative practice. Collaborative or social learning is also an important factor of CLIL learning (Martínez, 2011). When students engage in MOOC or classroom based discussions, "learning is promoted as participants share their views with peers, interact with the reading material and participate during sessions" (Viswanathan, 2012 cited in de Waard, 2015, n.p.).

2.3. Learning for the future

The actions taken by the students (e.g. choosing how to engage with online resources) prepares them for lifelong learning. MOOCs enable learners to use multiple sources to reach their learning goals (de Waard, 2015). This means that the ability to independently and proactively engage in behavioural processes to increase goal attainment becomes necessary (Zimmerman, 2000). As mentioned by de Waard (2015), "[a] study focusing on [SRL] conducted by Gutiérrez-Rojas et al. (2014, [p. 47]) showed that it is crucial to identify the lack of study skills and work habits as a significant factor, hindering the successful completion of MOOCs by less experienced learners" (n.p.). For this reason, an off-the-shelf instrument was used in our study in ways outlined below, to monitor and measure SRL: the Motivated Strategies for Learning Questionnaire (MSLQ) constructed by Pintrich, Smith, Garcia, and McKeachie (1991).

The emergence of MOOCs affords universities the "opportunity to provide students with preparatory courses before they enter university, at relatively low cost" (Jiang et al., 2014, p. 2). But in order for 5th grade secondary students to be able to quickly pick up the content and interaction opportunities provided in these MOOCs, researchers must understand whether pre-university students benefit from MOOCs, and what their specific challenges might be. For this reason, this study will investigate the effects of language, peer learning, and SRL coming from following MOOCs integrated in CLIL courses.

2.4. Research questions

Based on the literature, the following research questions were formulated:

- How do MOOCs impact CLIL learners when used in the CLIL classroom?

- Does learning from MOOCs add to their language learning?

- What is the effect of social learning (peer learning) on CLIL learners?

- Does MOOC learning increase critical learning skills?

- Does MOOC learning impact self-regulated learning?

3. Methodology

3.1. The MOOC-CLIL project

The MOOC-CLIL project pioneers the combination of both MOOC and CLIL concepts, and as such it is an exploratory study. It was important to use a mixed methods approach, including quantitative data concerning learning, and qualitative data to ensure a correct interpretation of the quantitative data. The quantitative data indicated where the learning was situated looking at the results coming from the MSLQ. The MSLQ was adapted to focus on relevant online learning elements[3]. The questions were put into sub-groups, following the grouping as suggested in Pintrich et al. (1991), and elaborated with questions probing critical online learning factors. The adapted questionnaire consisted of 50 questions, with multiple questions on intrinsic motivation, extrinsic motivation, course value, self-efficacy and learning performance, critical thinking, social learning (peer learning, help seeking), and learning self-awareness.

---

3. https://drive.google.com/file/d/0B2GekloYrdFQS0N3TGdtUnJCNmM/view

Chapter 4

The participants were asked to fill in the online survey prior to the MOOC-CLIL courses and in April (after the EigenMOOC phase, further discussed below). The semi-structured focus group interviews were set up per class in May 2016. The groups were limited to nine students to ensure all students could voice their experiences and this resulted in five focus groups.

The students' learning performance (e.g. language use, interactions, critical thinking, digital skills, cultural sensitivity) was also monitored through teacher-student mentoring. The evaluation consisted of a series of brief evaluations throughout the year (student feedback on the process, activities, and teachers) and evaluations by the teachers using an adapted Skills and Attitudes Measuring (SAM) scale[4].

3.2. Situating the project

The project ran during the 2015-2016 academic year, with a learning/teaching frequency of two hours per week. The MOOC-CLIL courses were part of 'vrije ruimte' (translated: free space), a course option providing innovative learning techniques to students. By using this course option, the content was not restricted, as the 'vrije ruimte' is not part of the mandatory course curriculum.

3.2.1. Target population

During the first MOOC introductory lesson, those students who wanted to volunteer for the MOOC-CLIL research were given an informed consent form with information on the research. All students signed the informed consent form.

The 42 secondary students in this pilot project were 5th grade secondary school students, all 16-17 years old. They were enrolled in those curricula that normally result in college or university entrance. All of their data was anonymised.

---

4. https://drive.google.com/file/d/0B2GekloYrdFQU18zbDhubE8tcDg/view

3.2.2. Three phases to scaffold autonomous learning

The project consisted of three phases: a GroupMOOC phase (collaboratively looking at the MOOC structure and elements), an EigenMOOC phase (students start to choose and follow MOOCs of their own preference), and a recapturing/production phase (groups of students produced their own MOOC video for next year's 5th graders).

In the GroupMOOC phase, all the students first took an introductory trajectory set out by the teachers that allowed the students to explore MOOC platforms and be introduced to the different learning activities and media options. The MOOC chosen for the English MOOC-CLIL group was the *Rise of Superheroes and Their Impact on Pop Culture*[5] offered through the edX platform, and for the French MOOC group an introduction to the *French school television platform*[6] was chosen. In this stage, the flipped classroom approach was used, providing students with specific MOOC elements followed by performing activities in class (e.g. debate, discussion, and analysing and selecting content). In the GroupMOOC phase, the teachers offered support in terms of language (e.g. indicating which online dictionaries could be used, what was meant by specific MOOC tasks or media).

In the second phase, EigenMOOC, the students chose their own MOOC. During EigenMOOC, the learners increasingly self-regulated their learning. They planned what to learn, how, and when.

In the recapturing phase, students produced a video collaboratively, combining all they had seen (e.g. what is a MOOC, which language activities were used). The videos were used to inform future 5th graders about the MOOC-CLIL courses. The students scripted, edited and narrated the movies themselves[7].

---

5. https://www.edx.org/course/rise-superheroes-impact-pop-culture-smithsonianx-popx1-5x

6. http://education.francetv.fr/

7. One of the movies can be viewed at https://www.youtube.com/watch?v=vFc1bZOelQs&feature=youtu.be

4. Findings

The findings below come from the online surveys (percentages) and the focus group interviews. The findings showed that most students were intrinsically motivated. As the project was rolled out, more students became aware of their actual learning capacities and their authentic language use increased. We also found that more students started to learn from peers, increased their critical thinking, and gained self-regulated learning skills.

4.1. Intrinsic versus extrinsic motivation

Overall, the students were more intrinsically (73%) than extrinsically motivated (35%), and the interviews suggested that this came from the freedom to choose what they wanted to learn: "the fact that I can learn something that I am truly interested in makes me want to learn at home as well" (ST18). The extrinsic motivation decreased as they became more aware of the freedom they had within the class, and grades became less important (44%) than learning something new (100% importance).

4.2. More realistic learning awareness

When comparing the results from both MSLQs, some of the self-regulated percentages of the questionnaire had decreased (see Table 1).

Table 1. Comparing percentages related to learning beliefs and learning self-awareness coming from the first and second round of the MSLQ

Survey learning topics	Results 1st survey	Results 2nd survey
Learning beliefs	85%	80%
Learning self-awareness	70%	69%

Comparing results from both MSLQs indicated that the students' learning beliefs (i.e. feeling confident that their learning actions were successful) had decreased and their learning self-awareness (i.e. becoming conscious of the learning they do) was hardly affected. However, the interviews revealed that the participants had become more aware of their learning capacity, realising they were not as knowledgeable as they had first expected (and indicated). It was this increased awareness that made their second survey percentages representative of what they actually felt performance-wise.

4.3. Language learning

During the interviews, all the students reported a dramatic increase in daring to speak either French or English, referring to language proficiency and motivation:

> "the best thing about the course is that I dare to express myself, without being scared" (ST2).

This was substantiated by feedback from the teachers based on the students' active language use within the classroom. The students emphasised the importance of speaking another language for two hours straight every week, and immersing themselves in topics with a vocabulary related to their own interests. All students felt that they used language more proficiently and authentically. They found the vocabulary they picked up also enriched regular language classes.

The English MOOC-CLIL students saw English as a major asset: "it is a global language" (ST13). 83% of students found they were now capable of expressing themselves autonomously in English or French. Participants reported that the MOOC media design allowed them to slow down videos, read transcripts of the content and select those media that they preferred (e.g. video or texts). However, some of the MOOC content was too complex to fully understand which was at times demotivating.

4.4. Social learning

Seeking help decreased from 71% of respondents at the commencement of the course to 60% at its completion. The answers to the questionnaires revealed a shift in help-seeking focus, moving from the teacher to peers (see Table 2).

Table 2. Percentages on help-seeking from both MSLQs

Survey learning topics	Results 1st survey	Results 2nd survey
Help-seeking (any)	71%	60%
Help-seeking from teacher	75%	59%
Help-seeking from peers	61%	83%

During the interviews, students indicated they were relying on the teacher's knowledge to get started ("the teacher gave us links to online language dictionaries which were very useful" (ST9)), but that after the first few weeks they only needed the teachers' help for specific MOOC task descriptions.

The interviews revealed enthusiasm for peer learning and connecting with global peers: "someone actually liked a comment I wrote in the discussion threads!" (ST35). This was supported by the results from the questionnaires, in which 68% gained knowledge by interacting with peers. The participants also indicated that social learning extended to learning to communicate respectfully, plan learning (sharing expertise with classmates), and improve critical thinking through discussions with classmates.

4.5. Critical thinking

The survey questions on critical thinking revealed that 63% of the students carefully considered what they were learning: "I now understand that I need to reflect on the content that is provided and whether this seems to be real or fake" (ST26). Students also trusted content coming from those MOOCs coming across as professional (good language use, comprehensible content). Online empathy (i.e. awareness of staying respectful in online discussions) rose from 93% to 100%, as students understood the language factor of potentially misunderstanding others (see Table 3).

Table 3. Evolution in critical thinking and online empathy from both MSLQs

Survey learning topics	Results 1st survey	Results 2nd survey
Critical thinking	55%	63%
Online empathy	93%	100%

4.6. Self-regulated learning

Increasingly, more students indicated they became more capable of digesting complex content, and more students started planning their learning one week ahead (see Table 4). The students became more critically aware of how content was delivered – language and content wise – which made them select more qualitatively strong MOOCs. More students felt the benefit of planning their learning: "MOOCs give an overview of the material in advance... it makes it easier to learn ahead of time as I know what is coming up and when" (ST39).

Table 4. Comparing percentages on SRL from both MSLQs

Survey learning topics	Results 1st survey	Results 2nd survey
Understanding complex content	35%	50%
Planning one week ahead	10%	19%

4.7. Sustainability of the project

By the end of the EigenMOOC phase, 72% of the students had independently started to follow a MOOC in their spare time. As the students were enthusiastic and showed an increase in their language skills (based on the SAM scale feedback), the school decided to deploy this approach in the years to come, increasing the number of students that could choose this type of class. At the start of the 2016-2017 academic year, 82 students enrolled in MOOC-CLIL.

5. Conclusions

Improved use of the foreign language in informal settings was a key learning outcome of this project: daring to speak and communicate with peers inside classrooms and MOOCs. As a result, students prepared for their futures, developed specific vocabulary in a professional area of their interest, and also became more efficient in planning their own learning and appreciating the benefits of peer and social learning.

This study proved once more that an exploratory study benefits from using a mixed methods approach, as qualitative vignettes from participants were used to provide additional substance to the quantitative element of the study. If the study had relied solely on the adapted MSLQ, the results (e.g. capacity to self-regulate learning) could have been misinterpreted due to lack of understanding behind those numbers (the students re-evaluating their capacity to learn to fit realistic assumptions).

6. Acknowledgements

We extend our deepest gratitude to all the students and teachers involved (Bjorn Vandewaetere and Mieke Anckaert), as well as the directors of the upper secondary level at GUSCO (Heidi Steegen and Nicole Casteele).

A special thank you to Professor Allison Littlejohn (The Open University) for bringing the MSLQ to our attention.

References

Bishop, J. L., & Verleger, M. A. (2013). The flipped classroom: a survey of the research. *Proceedings of the ASEE National Conference, Atlanta, GA*. https://www.asee.org/public/conferences/20/papers/6219/download

Bruff, D. O., Fisher, D. H., McEwen, K. E., & Smith, B. E. (2013). Wrapping a MOOC: student perceptions of an experiment in blended learning. *MERLOT Journal of Online Learning and Teaching, 9*(2), 187-199.

De Waard, I. (2015). MOOC factors influencing teachers in formal education. *Revista Mexicana de Bachillerato a distancia, 7*(13), 1-8.

De Waard, I., Abajian, S., Gallagher, M. S., Hogue, R., Keskin, N., Koutropoulos, A., & Rodriguez, O. C. (2011). Using mLearning and MOOCs to understand chaos, emergence, and complexity in education. *The International Review of Research in Open and Distance Learning, 12*(7), 94-115. https://doi.org/10.19173/irrodl.v12i7.1046

De Waard, I., Kukulska-Hulme, A., & Sharples, M. (2015). Investigating self-directed learning dimensions: adapting the Bouchard framework. In *Design for Teaching and Learning in a Networked World* (pp. 395-400). Springer International Publishing. https://doi.org/10.1007/978-3-319-24258-3_30

Dooly, M. (2008). *Telecollaborative language learning: a guidebook to moderating intercultural collaboration online*. Peter Lang.

Grover, S., Pea, R., & Cooper, S. (2014, March). Promoting active learning & leveraging dashboards for curriculum assessment in an OpenEdX introductory CS course for middle school. In *Proceedings of the first ACM conference on Learning@ scale conference* (pp. 205-206). ACM.

Gutiérrez-Rojas, I., Alario-Hoyos, C., Pérez-Sanagustín, M., Leony, D., & Delgado-Kloos, C. (2014). Scaffolding self-learning in MOOCs. *Proceedings of the Second MOOC European Stakeholders Summit, EMOOCs* (pp. 43-49).

Guzdial, M. (2014). Limitations of MOOCs for computing education-addressing our needs: MOOCs and technology to advance learning and learning research. *Magazine Ubiquity, 2014*(July), 1. https://doi.org/10.1145/2591683

Ho, A. D., Chuang, I., Reich, J., Coleman, C. A., Whitehill, J., Northcutt, C. G., William, J. J., Hansen, J. D., Lopez, G., & Petersen, R. (2015). *Harvardx and mitx: two years of open online courses fall 2012-summer 2014*. https://doi.org/10.2139/ssrn.2586847

Jiang, S., Williams, A. E., Warschauer, M., He, W., & O'Dowd, D. K. (2014). Influence of incentives on performance in a pre-college biology MOOC. *The International Review of Research in Open and Distributed Learning, 15*(5). https://doi.org/10.19173/irrodl.v15i5.1858

Liu, F., & Cavanaugh, C. (2012). Factors influencing student academic performance in online high school algebra. *Open Learning: The Journal of Open, Distance and e-Learning, 27*(2), 149-167. https://doi.org/10.1080/02680513.2012.678613

Marsh, D. (2002). *CLIL/EMILE-The European dimension: actions, trends and foresight potential*. European Union Report.

Martínez, M. R. P. (2011). CLIL and cooperative learning. *Encuentro 20*, 109-118.

Najafi, H., Evans, R., & Federico, C. (2014). MOOC integration into secondary school courses. *The International Review Of Research In Open And Distributed Learning, 15*(5). https://doi.org/10.19173/irrodl.v15i5.1861

Pellegrino, E., De Santo, M., & Vitale, G. (2013). Integrating learning technologies and autonomy: a CLIL course in Linguistics. *Procedia-Social and Behavioral Sciences, 106*, 1514-1522.

Pintrich, P. R., Smith, D., Garcia, T., & McKeachie, W. (1991). *A manual for the use of the motivated strategies for learning questionnaire (MSLQ)*. Ann Arbor, MI: The University of Michigan.

Scott, D., & Beade, S. (2014). *Improving the effectiveness of language learning: CLIL and computer-assisted language learning. Report for the European Commission, Education and Training* (pp. 1-36). London, UK: Watling House.

Viswanathan, R. (2012). Teaching and learning through MOOC. *Frontiers of Language and Teaching, 3*, 32-40.

Zimmerman, B. J. (2000). Attainment of self-regulation: a social cognitive perspective. In M. Boekaerts, P. R. Pintrich, & M. Zeidner (Eds), *Handbook of self-regulation* (pp. 13-39). San Diego: Academic Press. https://doi.org/10.1016/B978-012109890-2/50031-7

5 Dualism-based design of the Introductory Chinese MOOC 'Kit de contact en langue chinoise'

Jue Wang-Szilas[1] and Joël Bellassen[2]

Abstract

This article reviews the existing Chinese language Massive Open Online Courses (MOOCs) and points out three problems in their design: the monism-based teaching method, the non-integration of cultural elements, and the lack of learner-learner interactions. It then presents the design principles of the Introductory Chinese MOOC in an attempt to tackle these problems.

Keywords: teaching Chinese as a foreign language, MOOC, French-speaking Chinese learner, character-based teaching method.

1. Introduction

In 2013, the National Institute of Oriental Languages and Civilizations (INALCO, France) launched the project *Les MOOC de l'INALCO* using the French MOOC platform *France Université Numérique* (FUN). Chinese was one of the nine languages involved in this project, and the course was scheduled to start in November 2016. The authors of this paper are the authors of the Introductory Chinese MOOC.

---

1. University of Geneva, Geneva, Switzerland; jue.wangszilas@unige.ch

2. Institut National des Langues et Civilisations Orientales, Paris, France; joelbellassen@gmail.com

How to cite this chapter: Wang-Szilas, J., & Bellassen, J. (2017). Dualism-based design of the Introductory Chinese MOOC 'Kit de contact en langue chinoise'. In Q. Kan & S. Bax (Eds), *Beyond the language classroom: researching MOOCs and other innovations* (pp. 43-57). Research-publishing.net. https://doi.org/10.14705/rpnet.2017.mooc2016.670

Chapter 5

Chinese is a non-alphabetic language with many unique features. It is a tonal and non-inflectional language (verbs, nouns, articles, etc.) with a logographic writing system. The written language does not have direct correspondence with the sounds. Pinyin, the Romanization system of Chinese characters, helps to pronounce the characters and thus is helpful for aural and oral communication. However, just knowing Pinyin is not enough to understand Chinese. Besides, a word in Chinese can be a single character, two characters, or three characters, etc. So in what way could a Chinese MOOC teach those features to benefit the learners? In this article, we will first analyse some existing Chinese language MOOCs and then present how our MOOC attempted to address their shortcomings.

2. Review of some Chinese language MOOCs

Before and during the design of our MOOC, we reviewed the following Chinese language MOOCs in terms of the target learners, pedagogical approach to teaching characters, integration of cultural elements, and learner-learner interaction:

- *Chinese for beginners* of Beijing University (Coursera) https://www.coursera.org/learn/learn-chinese;

- *Mandarin Chinese: Start talking with 1.3 billion people* of Tsinghua University (edX) https://www.edx.org/course/tsinghua-chinese-start-talking-1-3-tsinghuax-tm01x;

- *Chinese Language: Learn Basic Mandarin* of Taiwan National Chengchi University (edX) https://www.edx.org/course/basic-mandarin-chinese-level-1-mandarinx-mx101x-0;

- *Intermediate Chinese Grammar* of Beijing University (edX) https://www.edx.org/course/zhong-ji-yi-yu-yu-fa-intermediate-pekingx-20000001x-0;

- *Chinese for HSK* series of Beijing University (Coursera) https://www.coursera.org/learn/hsk-1;

- *Chinese Characters for Beginners* of Peking University (Coursera) https://www.coursera.org/learn/hanzi.

2.1. Target learners

Most MOOCs that teach Chinese language are designed for English speakers as their target learners, including the ones listed above. The Introductory Chinese MOOC *Kit de contact en langue chinoise* is the first Chinese MOOC for French-speaking learners.

2.2. Pedagogical approach

These MOOCs vary greatly in their pedagogical approaches. The *Chinese for beginners* of Beijing University (Coursera), a typical xMOOC, focuses on knowledge transfer. This introductory course uses a traditional transmissive teaching approach with only one tutor giving lectures about Chinese language, without even one dialogue. The whole course was delivered in English with slides in Pinyin instead of Chinese characters.

The *Mandarin Chinese: Start talking with 1.3 billion people* of Tsinghua University (edX) and the *Chinese Language: Learn Basic Mandarin* of Taiwan National Chengchi University (edX) could be regarded as communication-based MOOCs.

The former focuses on daily basic language skills for everyday life in Mandarin speaking countries, particularly for foreign students in China. The dialogues are taught mostly in Pinyin, with very few frequently used characters. The latter aims to train the learners to be *competent* Chinese speakers as tourists to Taiwan. The vocabulary learning focuses on the usage of the words. Character teaching is not a priority in either course. Both MOOCs have interesting dialogues with different scenarios to help develop learners' communicative skills.

The other three MOOCs in the list teach specific skills of the Chinese language. The *Intermediate Chinese Grammar* of Beijing University (edX) focuses on the intensive learning of Chinese grammar. The *Chinese for HSK* series of Beijing University (Coursera) is for the HSK test preparation, which to some extent could be viewed as an online resource, and the *Chinese Characters for Beginners* of Peking University (Coursera) focuses on character teaching, but with no supporting words or dialogues to help memorize the taught characters.

3. Learner-learner interaction and integration of culture

There are limited learner-learner interactions in the discussion forums for all of the above MOOCs. The communications are not interactive as learners only post their views without interacting with other learners. They do it either to finish that task so they can proceed to the next step or simply to establish their online presence.

Regarding the integration of the Chinese culture with language teaching, we feel that few cultural elements are integrated in the teaching of dialogues, language activities and forum discussions.

In summary, we can see that the teacher-centered and knowledge-based approaches are still dominant in the field. In our opinion, these MOOCs fail to address the following three fundamental questions in their design:

- What is the basic teaching unit, character or word, especially for beginners? And how is this basic unit presented in the design of a MOOC in Chinese?

- How to design activities that promote learner-learner interactions?

- How to promote intercultural learning in a Chinese language MOOC?

4. Literature review

4.1. Monism vs dualism

Since Teaching Chinese as a Foreign Language (TCFL) became an academic discipline in the 1980's (Lü, 1987), educators and researchers have been debating over the basic unit of teaching Chinese language. During the 1980's and 90's, the debate was mainly between the word-based teaching method (词本位) and character-based or Zi-based teaching method (字本位).

The word-based method can be traced back to Ma (1898) who wrote the first Chinese grammar book, advocating words as the basic units of language teaching. Under the influence of this approach, most existing Chinese language teaching materials have been designed to teach the word first, then use the words to make sentences, and finally the composition of the text, which is similar to the methods used in the teaching of English, French, and other phonetic languages.

The character-based teaching method (Lu, 2011; Pan, 2002; Ren, 2002; Wang, 2000; Wang, 2009; Xu, 1997, 2005) regarded Chinese characters as the basic unit of teaching, but at the same time acknowledging the strong connection between characters and words (Bellassen, 2016). It argued that teaching should respect the unique characteristics of Chinese languages (as mentioned before). It emphasized the character-based theory in Chinese Language Studies in that characters are the basic building blocks of Chinese syntax, just as words are that of Indo-European languages (Shen, 2016).

During recent years, the terms *character-based* and *word-based* have caused some misunderstanding and confusion. The two terms, originally used to distinguish two main teaching methods, were put in sharp opposition to each other by some Chinese linguists.As such, Bellassen (2016) recently proposed the concepts of *dualism* (二元论) and *monism* (一元论). For him, the *monism-based method* regards words as the basic teaching units and that the character teaching should follow the teaching of words. However, the *dualism-based method* admits the existence of two basic units of Chinese teaching: character and word. The character teaching should guide the word teaching so as to make learning efficient, especially for beginners. What is more, the *dualism-based method* emphasizes the development of the visual identification of graphics and thus improves the memorization of characters.

The MOOCs reviewed above were designed with *monism-based method*s, hence the memorization of characters was neglected.

4.2. Positioning of cultural elements

It is widely accepted that language and culture are inseparable in language teaching. We think that the cultural elements should not be a simple knowledge transfer. The integration of cultural elements would enforce and enrich language learning and play a very important role in motivating learner participation and stimulating critical thinking (Álvarez & Kan, 2012). The question is, how can we embed it in the MOOC design to encourage critical thinking and intercultural learning.

4.3. Learner-learner interaction

Interaction is a central focus in language learning, especially for an online massive language course. The timely feedback from teachers and peer students plays a very important role in a MOOC for language learning (Lin & Zhang, 2014). As we have mentioned beforehand, most of the interactions observed in the above mentioned MOOCs were not interactive. The role of interactions should go beyond the level of providing correct answers by creating collaborative problem-solving experiences that "empower learners in networked environments for fostering critical thinking and collaboration, developing competence based outcomes, encouraging peer assistance and assessment through social appraisal, providing strategies and tools for self-regulation, and finally using a variety of media and ICTs to create and publish learning resources and outputs" (Guàrdia, Maina, & Sangrà, 2013, p. 1).

In the next section, we will present how we applied the above three principles in the design of our MOOC.

5. Design of the Introductory Chinese MOOC

5.1. Course structure and objective

The Introductory Chinese MOOC, a seven week MOOC, is designed to teach beginners' Chinese to French-speaking learners who have no or little knowledge of Chinese language and culture. It aims to help learners develop personalized strategies to learn a 'distant language' such as Chinese, and finally to facilitate their discovery of the Chinese culture (https://www.fun-mooc.fr/courses/Inalco/52004/session1/about).

Except for the introductory week, each of the following weeks centers around character teaching accompanied by a variety of simple topic-based tasks. Each week ends with a culture session where one or two cultural elements are introduced and open ended questions are asked.

The learning outcomes are comparable to A1 of the Common European Framework of Reference for languages (CEFR). At the end of the course, learners were required to master 100 high frequency characters[3].

5.2. Dualism-based teaching method

The design of the MOOC is guided by a dualism-based teaching method (Bellassen & Zhang, 1989), with careful consideration taken with the unique characteristics of the Chinese language and the French-speaking learners' specific difficulties, i.e. to establish the link between the character, its romanized Pinyin, and the tone (Figure 1).

The design focus of the learning activities was to establish the *character-meaning-sound* link that did not exist in French. From the perspective of the dualism-based method, this dimension could be emphasized with the use of

---

3. The 100 high frequency characters were chosen on the basis of the Table of 400 characters, an index to characters, in Bellassen and Zhang's (1989) book.

Chapter 5

technology to increase the learners' exposure to the characters and words and thus help to memorize them (Figure 2).

Figure 1. Lecture videos of the Introductory Chinese MOOC

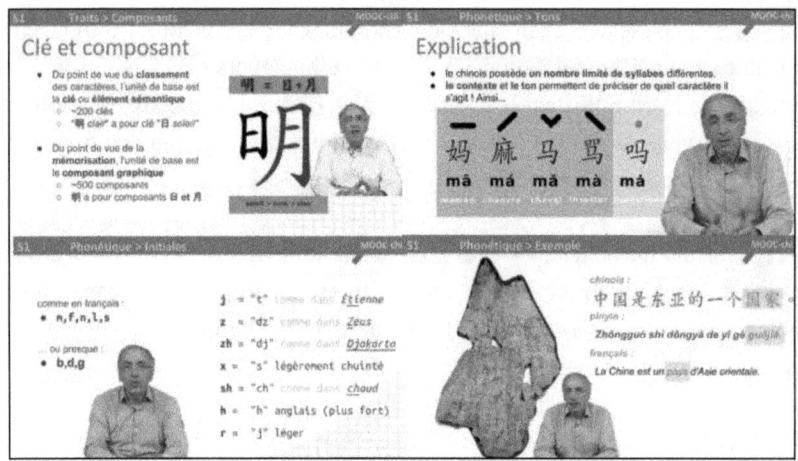

Figure 2. The design of character-meaning-sound learning activities

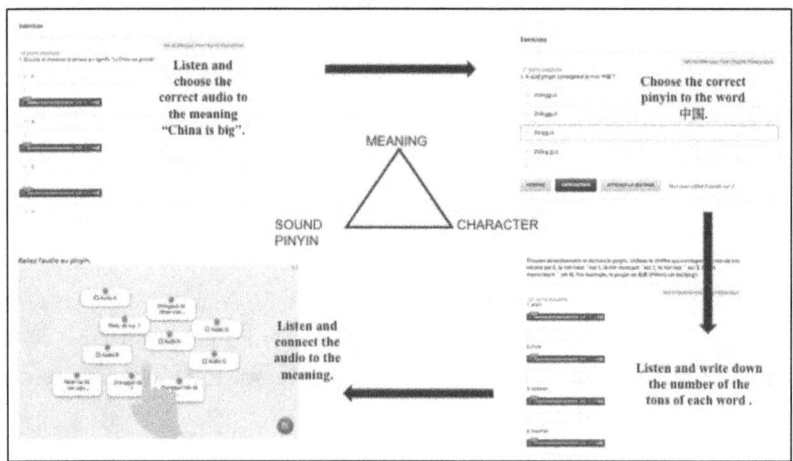

Due to limited tools on the FUN platform, different types of learning activities were introduced to the MOOC:

- aural reception (distinguish phonetics);

- aural comprehension (understand the content of a dialogue or a text);

- oral practice (repeat with an audio);

- visual practice (distinguish characters);

- hand-writing practice (write characters on paper with teacher presentation);

- reading comprehension (understand a text);

- writing (type in Chinese with a computer).

These activities were categorized as *assessable* and *non-assessable*. The quizzes created within the platform FUN were *assessable* activities, usually after lecture videos. The interactive learning games created with the external tools could not be evaluated by the platform FUN for technical reasons. These games, together with phonetic practice and character handwriting practice, were introduced as *non-assessable* activities. However, there was a strong link between them (Figure 3) so that the learners were obliged to do all these activities to reach a passing score.

5.3. Learner-learner interaction

As mentioned earlier, the fostering of learner autonomy and critical thinking were considered as vital in the success of a language MOOC. A forum, as a very important online interaction tool, was introduced with different purposes in the design of the Introductory Chinese MOOC.

Chapter 5

There were 49 forums created in the present MOOC, falling into two main types: experience sharing and critical thinking development. The experience sharing forums were created after some *non-assessable* games or exercises, aiming not only to encourage peer assistance, to share learning strategies and experiences, thus to foster collaboration, but also to develop reflective learning processes (Figure 4).

Figure 3. The link between assessable and non-assessable exercises

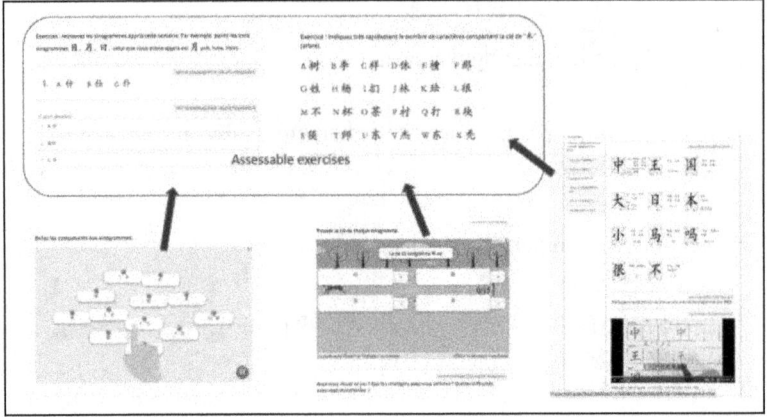

Figure 4. Discussion forum for non-assessable exercises

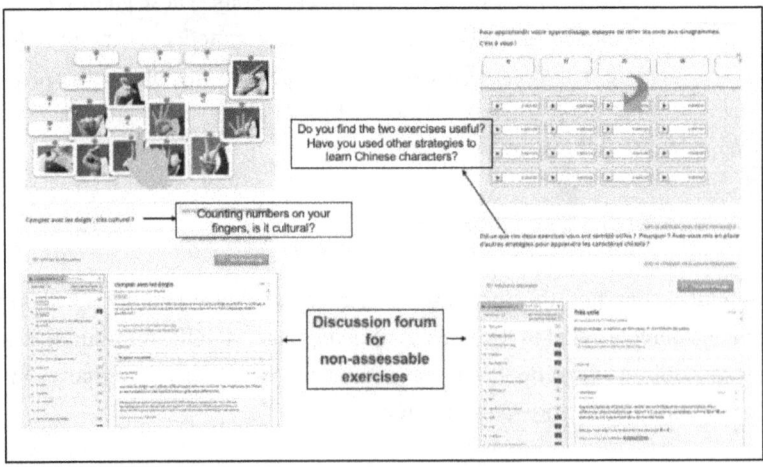

5.4. Embedding culture to develop critical thinking

Each week, the learning ended with a culture session. The cultural elements were very carefully selected to make sure that they were relevant to the language content of that week. It aimed to both expand cultural knowledge and develop critical thinking, thus promoting learner motivation. Take the cultural session of Week 2 as an example; after watching the video about the population of China, the learners were encouraged to exchange their views in a discussion about 'the great inner migration during the Chinese New Year period' (Figure 5).

Figure 5. Discussion forum in Week 2 for the culture session

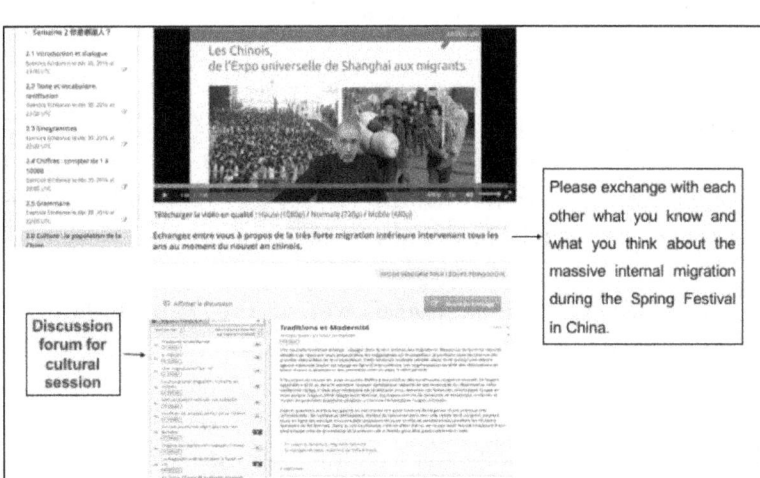

There were more than 670 posts in the forum. The discussion, entitled 'Tradition and Modernity', attracted 30 responses. The student who posted the first message commented on the common phenomenon that instead of following the tradition of going home to spend the Chinese New Year with their parents, more and more young people invite their parents to come to the cities where they work to spend the festival, but the tradition of giving 'red envelopes' (new year money) to children is kept. In the responses, some students thanked the first poster for sharing this information; "Merci pour toutes ces informations passionnantes". Some compared it to what they had experienced in China and other countries, for example, in Japan, 'red envelopes' are given to even 20 year old young people; "Au Japon également il y a cette tradition de donner une enveloppe avec de l'argent (お年玉) mais ceci jusqu'à la majorité ! (20 ans)". A lot of students expressed their appreciation in the discussion thread that sharing various views helped them deepen their understanding of Chinese language and culture; "j'apprends petit à petit à la connaître au travers des vidéos des cours, mais aussi grâce aux informations et expériences que partagent les participants du forum".

6. Evaluation and conclusion

At the end of the course, the participants were invited to take a post-course questionnaire. 296 completed responses were obtained, about 10% of the active learners (2,827 of 9,805 registered learners). It can not be regarded as representative for all active learners, but may give us some indications to improve the MOOC (see Table 1).

The general feedback from the learners was positive. Most of them (96%) claimed that the MOOC met their personal expectations and the course content and organization were satisfactory (95%). On average, about 90% of learners participated in more than 3/4 of the MOOC, and 93% of them obtained the certificate. However, technical problems, lack of time, and workplace commitments were considered as the main barriers in completing the MOOC.

Table 1. Key results from post-course questionnaires

Question	Answer
I am satisfied with the MOOC	97%
I have attained my learning objectives	96%
I am satisfied with the content of the MOOC	95%
On average, I spent ____ hours per week following the MOOC 1-3h 3-5 5-8	 28% 39% 23%

I have met these difficulties in following the MOOC	
technical problems (Internet, software, MOOC platform)	41%
lack of time	31%
work obligations	26%
I participated in at least ¾ of the following activities (>3/4)	90%
watching videos	96%
doing exercises	96%
playing games	95%
practising handwriting	78%
reading forum posts	45%
Participating in forum discussions	25%
I think the following interaction(s) was(were) of help for my learning	
with tutors	48%
with other learners	48%
with all kinds of learning activities	89%
I think the interaction with other learners helped me to enrich my knowledge	63%
understand well the content of the MOOC	27%
guide my learning	25%
I obtained the certificate for the purpose of personal satisfaction	54%
including it in my CV	34%
looking for a job	4%

We were especially pleased by learners' dynamic participation in learner-learner interactions. In the 49 forums created in this MOOC, there were 4,305 discussion threads, without counting the number of posts in one thread of discussion. To be particularly noted, the total posts in the seven week culture section forums reached 3,386. The learners were very active not only in helping each other to learn Chinese language and culture, but also in helping the teachers improve the course.

The first experience of the Introductory Chinese MOOC, for both learners and teachers, will definitely help to ameliorate the course in the future. More visual games will be introduced because a lot of students found them quite efficient in helping them recognize and memorize Chinese characters, though they were not assessed. It will also be a good idea to integrate some recording tools in the platform so that the learners can submit, compare and evaluate their oral productions.

A big challenge for language MOOCs lies in practising the language with native speakers. Telecollaboration might be a good solution as language learners practise their target language with native speakers and both sides benefit. The eTandem Chinese-French course model (Wang-Szilas, 2016) has proved to have potential in helping language learners develop their communicative competences and intercultural competence. In the long run, it would be interesting to create an eTandem MOOC that can connect a Chinese MOOC for French-speaking learners and a French MOOC for Chinese-speaking learners so that they can practise the target languages with each other. This will definitely open a new research area for the design of language MOOCs.

7. Acknowledgements

The project was funded by l'Université Sorbonne Paris Cité with technical support from the TICE (Technologies de l'Information et de la Communication pour l'Enseignement) group of INALCO.

References

Álvarez, I., & Kan, Q. (2012). Supporting intercultural learning for beginners' Chinese language learners at the Open University, UK. In L. Jin & M. Cortazzi (Eds), *Researching intercultural learning: investigations in language and education* (pp. 209-234). Palgrave Macmillan.

Bellassen, J. (2016). 学科建设的重大认识论障碍. 中山大学外国语学院系列讲座之一 Major epistemological barriers in the disciplinary construction. One of a series of talks in the School of Foreign Languages Sun Yat-sen University.

Bellassen, J., & Zhang, P. (1989). 汉语语言文字启蒙. *Methode d'initiation à la langue et à l'écriture chinoises*. La Compagnie.

Guàrdia, L., Maina, M., & Sangrà, A. (2013). MOOC design principles: a pedagogical approach from the learner's perspective. *eLearning Papers, 33*. http://hdl.handle.net/10609/41681

Lin, C. H., & Zhang, Y. (2014). MOOCs and Chinese language education. *Journal of Technology and Chinese Language Teaching, 5*(2), 49-65.

Lu, J. M. 陆俭明. (2011). 我关于"字本位"的基本观点. 语言科学. My basic opinion on character-based approach. *Linguistic Science, 10*(3), 225-230.

Lü, B. S. 吕必松. (1987). 对外汉语教学的紧迫任务. 世界汉语教学, (1), 1-4. dui wai han yu jiao xue de jin po ren wu. The urgent mission for teaching Chinese as a foreign language. *Chinese Teaching in the World, 1987*(1), 1-4.

Ma, J. 马建忠. (1898). 马氏文通 Ma's Grammar. The Commercial Press.

Pan, W. G. 潘文国. (2002). 字本位与汉语研究 Character-centred theory and Chinese language studies. East China Normal University Press.

Ren, H. L. 任瑚琏. (2002). Zi and words: which is the basic unit in Chinese teaching and the teaching strategies. *Chinese Teaching in the World, 2012*(4), 112.

Shen, H. Y. (2016). The basic ideas of the character-based theory by Tongqiang Xu. *Studies in Literature and Language, 11*(4), 65-68.

Wang, J. 王骏. (2009). 字本位与对外汉语教学. 上海交通大学出版社. Character-based theory and teaching Chinese as a foreign language. Shanghai Jiaotong University Press.

Wang, R. J. 王若江. (2000). 由法国"字本位"汉语教材引发的思考. 世界汉语教学, (3), 89-98. you fa guo zi ben wei han yu jiao cai yin fa de si kao. Reflection on the French character-based Chinese textbook. *Chinese Teaching in the World, 2000*(3).

Wang-Szilas, J. (2016). *Les enjeux de l'intégration de l'eTandem en didactique des langues-cultures étrangères : interactions entre apprenants et dynamique institutionnelle dans un dispositif universitaire sino-francophone*. Doctoral dissertation. University of Geneva.

Xu, T. Q. 徐通锵. (1997). 语言论: 语义型语言的结构原理和研究方法. 东北师范大学出版社. Linguistic Theory: Structure Principles and Research Methods of Semantic Languages. Northeast Normal University Press.

Xu, T. Q. 徐通锵. (2005). "字本位"和语言研究. 语言教学与研究, 6, 001. zi ben wei he yu yan yan jiu. Character-based theory and language studies. *Language Teaching and Linguistic Studies, 2005*(6).

6. The Move-Me project: reflecting on xMOOC and cMOOC structure and pedagogical implementation

Laura McLoughlin[1] and Francesca Magnoni[2]

Abstract

This paper discusses the rationale and structure of two Massive Open Online Courses (MOOCs) created as part of the EU-funded Move-Me project, which aims to develop two MOOCs and open educational resources for university learners participating in mobility programmes in Europe. The MOOCs are designed to help learners develop the skills necessary to understand, critique and deploy academic discourse in selected disciplines. The article will first briefly present the Move-Me project, its objectives, and outcomes. It will then explain the methodological framework of reference for the two MOOCs, reflect on x, c, and hybrid MOOC structures and discuss how metacognitive skills and strategies are employed to achieve the stated learning objectives.

Keywords: Move-Me, language MOOC, academic English, academic Italian, student mobility, languages for specific purposes.

---

1. National University of Ireland, Galway, Ireland; laura.mcloughlin@nuigalway.ie

2. National University of Ireland, Galway, Ireland; francesca.magnoni@nuigalway.ie

How to cite this chapter: McLoughlin, L., & Magnoni, F. (2017). The Move-Me project: reflecting on xMOOC and cMOOC structure and pedagogical implementation. In Q. Kan & S. Bax (Eds), *Beyond the language classroom: researching MOOCs and other innovations* (pp. 59-69). Research-publishing.net. https://doi.org/10.14705/rpnet.2017.mooc2016.671

Chapter 6

1. Introduction

In summer 2015, the European Commission approved funding for the Move-Me project under the Erasmus+ programme, Key Activity 2 strand. This two-year project (November 2015-October 2017) is led by the Università per Stranieri di Siena (Italy) and the Consortium is made up of the National University of Ireland, Galway (Ireland), the Open University (United Kingdom), the Computer Technology Institute (Greece), the Federazione Nazionale Insegnanti (Italy) and the Institutul de Stiinte Ale Educatiei (Romania).

Move-Me (MOOCs for uniVErsity students on the Move in Europe) targets university students who take part in mobility study programmes and therefore need to be able to negotiate academic discourse in a second language. Whilst the project focuses on English and Italian for academic purposes, it also aims to deliver templates for future developments in other languages. Upon completion, Move-Me will deliver two MOOCs (one for English for academic purposes and one for Italian for academic purposes), a website (www.movemeproject. eu), and a set of resources for students taking part in Erasmus or other mobility programmes.

The Move-ME project addresses the needs of university students who travel to European or international institutions to attend courses in a second language. Whilst students participating in mobility programmes are normally expected to possess at least a B1 competence – in the Common European Framework of Reference (CEFR) framework – in the target language, in many cases, that competence is limited to standard communication contexts rather than discipline-specific academic discourse, something which can hamper their full and meaningful participation in academic life abroad.

The two MOOCs, currently being developed, will be delivered through the FutureLearn platform and introduce learners to the concept of academic discourse. They are both built around the same macro-structure in terms of theoretical framework, duration and overall learning objectives: enhancing and developing learning to learn skills in the context of academic discourse through reflection on metacognitive strategies and guided application of metacognitive skills. Both MOOCs include authentic expository texts from the same selection of disciplines: economics, law, linguistics, literature and science. The Move-Me MOOCs are not language courses, however they should be classified as language MOOCs as they help to improve transversal, lexical, syntactical and paralinguistic competences as well as intercultural textual competence, i.e. the ability to understand and structure academic texts consistent with the cultural and stylistic convention of the target language.

2. Methodological framework

As it is now widely known, George Siemens and Stephen Downes are credited with having created the first ever MOOC in 2008[3], which was soon followed by more massive online courses. These early MOOCs, delivered through collaborative tools, blogs and discussion boards rather than content/learning management systems, have come to be known as c-MOOCs. They are underpinned by the connectivist approach heralded by Siemens and Downes, and are characterised by a rather free structure, where participants manage their own time, resources and learning path.

This type of MOOC, however, requires participants to possess advanced fluency in digital literacies and competence in the so-called '21st century skills'. According to the Partnership for 21st Century Skills[4], such abilities include collaboration, creativity, communication, critical thinking and information media skills. cMOOCs participants need these skills in order to be able to share and gain knowledge while navigating the complexities of a non-linear online collaborative and connectivist environment. Without them, learners may encounter difficulties in building their knowledge.

---

3. http://www.downes.ca/post/57750

4. http://www.p21.org/

Chapter 6

In addition, cMOOCs, because of their very nature, make official certification of acquired knowledge particularly difficult. Cognitive load theory (Sweller, 1994; Paas, Renkl, & Sweller, 2003) however, indicates that learning paths should culminate in specific (and certifiable) outcomes so that appropriate support can be designed for the purpose of reaching such outcomes. xMOOCs more closely respond to this need. They are more 'behaviourist' in nature and put an emphasis on content rather than connections. xMOOCs tend to mirror more closely, in so far as that is possible, a traditional learning environment, and support more traditional literacies. The xMOOCs are so called because of "the open course model originally formed as MITx, which was then joined by other universities and has evolved into edX.org" (Sokolik, 2014, p. 18).

As MOOCs developed and rapidly became more widespread, the distinction between the two types was blurred. And indeed, Move-Me MOOCs can be classified as a hybrid between the two: they follow a linear structure divided into a number of sequential 'steps' (therefore following the xMOOC model), but they strongly support the development of digital and 21st century skills (which, in turn, positions them within cMOOCs). At the same time, possession of these skills by participants is not taken for granted, so the introductory week of the two MOOCs includes reflective tasks on the digital competences necessary for the successful completion of the courses. It is therefore important to present and explain them to participants. It was decided that a sequential structure was particularly suited to the content of our courses, as it more closely resembles the structure of language modules that university students are normally familiar with, therefore helping to lower the affective filter.

2.1. Macro-structure of the Move-Me MOOCs

In order to cover the four main language abilities, reading, listening, writing and speaking, and to provide an introduction and a conclusion to the course, Move-Me MOOCs are divided into 6 weeks. Week 1 and Week 6 are the introductory and the conclusive units of each course. Week 1 explains the aims and structure of the course, skills needed, and suggestions for progressing through the material presented. Week 6 sums up the work done, the strategies that were highlighted during the previous weeks, as well as the skills practised so far. It contains activities to encourage learners to become aware of their own learning style and evaluate their own learning also reflecting on their (hopefully) enhanced awareness of metacognitive strategies and skills and abilities to apply them.

Weeks 2 to 5 present a similar structure. Week 2 focuses on enhancing and refining *reading* skills, Week 3 on *listening* skills, Week 4 on *writing* skills and Week 5 on *speaking* skills. The content of each week is linked to the content of previous and/or subsequent weeks. Building familiarity with the content, and therefore gradually simplifying its understanding, is seen as a way of helping learners to focus more on *learning strategies*.

More specifically for the English MOOC, the activities in Week 2, 3, 4, and 5 encourage significant and highly contextualised interaction among learners, mainly based on their reflections on their own approach to studying subjects through the Target Language (TL). Links and cross-references to activities targeting metacognitive strategies in steps presented in other weeks offer an opportunity for deeper learning and show how the same strategies can be reused or integrated when working on different abilities. The four main language abilities are strictly interconnected and so are the strategies that help to develop them: for instance, global and selective reading strategies (i.e. skimming and scanning) are also related to certain bottom-up or top-down listening strategies (i.e. inferring and predicting, global understanding or listening for specific information); the writing ability involves high order thinking skills as well as visual processing of the text also present in reading. The visual impact of the written text facilitates mnemonic retention of lexical elements that can then be reused when speaking. The purposely tailored cross-reference between the various weeks described earlier aims to enhance learners' awareness of the learning strategies they activate in specific learning contexts[5].

---

[5]. Examples of inputs for the Forum or the Learning Journal for reflection on their own learning strategies plus an example of an activity to understand their own listening or reading skills: 1) when you read a paper, according to the definitions given, do you use a global or a selective reading? 2) When do you use one and when the other? 3) After having listened to this section, which strategy do you use more, bottom-up or top-down? Why? Why do you think the strategy you use more suits you best?

Material used in the MOOC was carefully selected: it was decided to use different extracts from the same videos to give unity and continuity to the Weeks (or units). The sequencing of abilities within the MOOC focuses on receptive abilities first (reading and listening) and productive abilities later (writing and speaking), as follows:

- Week 2: *reading*. Learners are introduced to an initial visual contact with the texts: they see the specific language and structures used in specific contexts (i.e. academic texts on the subjects they choose to study); meaningful, selected transcripts and subtitles of the chosen extract are provided.

- Week 3: *listening*. The material selected for this unit is strictly connected to the material presented in Week 2 and the types of activities recall – and possibly facilitate the reuse of – what was learnt the previous week and can now be applied in the current week.

- Week 4: *writing*. Activities in this week help to reinforce both linguistic competence and learners' awareness of how their own strategies work, and focus on exploring how such strategies can be optimised in written tasks.

- Week 5: *speaking*. This is arguably the most challenging ability to develop in an asynchronous online environment. Learners are asked to interact among themselves not only through the forum (in writing) but also by recording and sharing short podcasts in which they discuss academic topics.

The theoretical framework chosen as background for designing the macro- and the micro-structures of the two MOOCs, and the sequencing of abilities, is Bloom's taxonomy revised and adapted to a digital environment (Anderson & Krathwohl, 2001a). The original taxonomy arranged thinking skills on a scale which went from lower to higher order thinking skills as follows:

Lower Order -----------------> Higher Order

Knowledge – Comprehension – Application – Analysis – Synthesis – Evaluation

Anderson and Krathwohl's (2001b) revised taxonomy, instead, includes the following thinking skills:

Lower Order -----------------> Higher Order

Remembering – Understanding – Applying – Analysing – Evaluating – Creating

Starting from lower order thinking skills – remembering, understanding, applying – involved primarily, but not exclusively in Week 2 (reading) and Week 3 (listening), learners are gradually encouraged to develop and use higher order thinking skills – analysing, evaluating, creating – employed mainly, but again not solely, in Week 4 (writing) and Week 5 (speaking). Feedback is provided to learners through quizzes or tests that are self-assessed. The methodological framework for creating activities is the Task-Based model, to encourage learners to work on and with the TL and improve their linguistic competence with what Ellis (1995) defines as interpretation tasks:

> "An alternative approach to grammar teaching is to design activities that focus learners' attention on a targeted structure in the input and that enable them to identify and comprehend the meaning(s) of this structure. This approach emphasises input processing for comprehension rather than output processing for production and requires the use of what I have termed interpretation tasks to replace traditional production tasks [... Interpretation] is the process by which learners endeavour to comprehend input and in so doing pay attention to specific linguistic features and their meanings. It involves noticing and cognitive comparison and results in intake" (pp. 88-90).

Learners are therefore encouraged to process input through interpretation, reflecting on linguistic and paralinguistic features. This should lead to enhanced mnemonic retention of lexical and syntactical elements. However, the aim of the Move-Me MOOCs is not just the enhancement of linguistic competence but, as already stated, also the elicitation of the cognitive processes involved in language learning.

2.2. Micro-structure of the English MOOC

Within the overarching macro-structures which ensure consistency as well as adherence to the overall learning objectives of the MOOCs and of the Move-Me project in general, each week has a micro-structure with its own learning objective and internal cohesion as well as specific focus on chosen metacognitive skills and strategies. These metacognitive skills and strategies are selected in accordance with the Cognitive Academic Language Learning Approach (CALLA) devised by Chamot and O'Malley (1987, 1994). Metacognitive strategies "involve executive processes in planning for learning, monitoring one's comprehension and production, and evaluating how well one has achieved a learning objective" (Chamot & O'Malley, 1987, p. 241). More specifically, metacognitive strategies can be divided into:

> "**Advance organisation:** Previewing the main ideas and concepts of the material to be learned, often by skimming the text for the organising principle; **Organisational planning:** Planning the parts, sequence, main ideas, or language functions to be expressed orally or in writing; **Selective attention:** Deciding in advance to attend to specific aspects of input, often by scanning for key words, concepts, and/or linguistic markers; **Self-monitoring:** Checking one's comprehension during listening or reading or checking the accuracy and/or appropriateness of one's oral or written production while it is taking place" (Chamot & O'Malley, 1987, p. 248).

All the strategies mentioned by Chamot and O'Malley (1987) are employed in the MOOCs and particular attention is paid to self-monitoring, which "has been linked to productive language, in which learners correct themselves during speaking or writing [...] effective ESL listeners also use self-monitoring to check on how well they are comprehending an oral text" (Chamot & O'Malley, 1987, p. 243). With self-monitoring learners are more actively involved in the comprehension and learning tasks and with the self-evaluation process, they decide whether the learning task is achieved or whether they need revision.

Sequencing of activities within each week follows the revised taxonomy shown above with tasks aimed at leading learners to become aware, recognise and develop the most common cognitive strategies and apply them to reading, listening, writing and speaking in the TL. Although each week focuses on one skill, other skills are also practised – and awareness of intercultural specificity in linguistic elements is also stimulated, for example understanding and recognising different coding systems, register, intonation, tone, and ways of emphasising important information in discipline-specific contexts in different cultures.

Following the introduction to each week, the first input learners receive each week is an audio-visual input: a short video clip introduces the linguistic content which will form the main focus of that week. The inclusion in the MOOC of video, audio and written material is designed to appeal to different learner types, however the authors felt that videos should be positioned at the beginning of each week because they are engaging text types and can help to activate motivation, especially among the intended target group.

As the week develops, two essential tools become the main platform through which interaction and reflection takes place: a forum section and the Reflective Journal. Typical of MOOCs, the forum aims to create a community of learners who, for affinity of interests and purposes, should be willing to share experiences, ideas and comments using the TL, thereby involving both the emotional and the intellectual sphere. The Reflective Journal is an individual task, which institutions could recognise through awarding of European Credit Transfer and Accumulation System (ECTS) or other accreditation, and requires

Chapter 6

participants to write entries related to specific and guided input[6] and to interact in the Forum using the target foreign language.

Metacognitive strategies and skills are a significant part of the learning content of the Move-Me MOOCs: it is envisaged that making learners aware of their own learning strategies and style, while pragmatically and practically dealing with the foreign language and its structures and specific vocabulary in an academic context, will provide them the necessary tools to become autonomous learners. Ultimately, participants are guided towards understanding and appraising their reactions when faced with complex linguistic input relevant to their field of study. This, in turn, should lead participants towards a more efficient organisation of TL learning by stimulating an inclination to monitor their own learning process, enhancing their ability to combine this monitoring attitude with background discipline-specific or linguistic knowledge and improving confidence in reapplying metacognitive strategies.

3. Conclusion

Studying a discipline through a foreign language can be a daunting task for students who may well have acquired a good level of fluency in standard communication but may still lack the competence to tackle discipline-specific discourse, because quite often language courses at university level only cover standard communication and not necessarily or not extensively discipline-specific academic discourse. This competence, however, is needed if learners are to participate in and enjoy the benefits of academic life while on mobility. The emphasis that the Move-Me MOOCs put on the recognition and development of metacognitive skills is designed to help students develop the necessary tools to progress to more complex texts outside the confines of the MOOCs, and hopefully encourage them to take a more active part in their academic

---

6. Sample questions for the Reflective Journals are: What did you learn today? How will you use what we are learning outside the class? When you are about to try something new, how do you feel? When you are doing something and you get stuck, what do you do? Do you carry on normal daily activities (e.g. study, cook, relax, drive) the same way in every situation? Which is the most important ability for you? Why? Can we consider the four main abilities linked or separated one from the other? How will they help you while studying in a foreign university?

experience while abroad. As the MOOCs are currently being developed and will be piloted in 2017, data on participation and feedback is not available at the time of writing. Reports on the MOOCs and on the project will be available on www.movemeproject.eu on completion of the project. The website will also give access to material and resources developed for the MOOCs as well as guidelines and templates for the development of similar MOOCs in other languages and/ or other disciplines. It is hoped that the MOOCs will become part of university students' preparation for their mobility programmes and that they can eventually be formally incorporated into training and/or teaching modules.

References

Anderson, L. W., & Krathwohl, D. R. (2001a). *Bloom's taxonomy revised: understanding the new version of Bloom's taxonomy.* http://thesecondprinciple.com/teaching-essentials/beyond-bloom-cognitive-taxonomy-revised/

Anderson, L. W., & Krathwohl, D. R. (Eds). (2001b). *A taxonomy for learning, teaching, and assessing: a revision of Bloom's taxonomy of educational objectives.* Boston, MA: Pearson Education Group.

Chamot, A. U., & O'Malley, J. M. (1987). The cognitive academic language learning approach: a bridge to the mainstream Author(s). *TESOL Quarterly, 21*(2), 227-249. https://doi.org/10.2307/3586733

Chamot, A. U., & O'Malley, J. M. (1994). *The CALLA handbook: implementing the cognitive academic language learning approach.* Addison-Wesley Publishing Company.

Ellis, R. (1995). Interpretation tasks for grammar teaching. *TESOL, 29*(1), 87-104. https://doi.org/10.2307/3587806

Paas, F., Renkl, A., & Sweller, J. (2003). Cognitive load theory and instructional design: recent developments. *Educational Psychologist, 38*(1), 1-4. https://doi.org/10.1207/S15326985EP3801_1

Sokolik, M. (2014). What constitutes an effective language MOOC? In E. Martín-Monje & E. (Eds), *Language MOOCs: providing learning, transcending boundaries.* Warsaw/Berlin: De Gruyter Open. https://doi.org/10.2478/9783110420067.2

Sweller, J. (1994). Cognitive load theory, learning difficulty, and instructional design. *Learning and Instruction, 4,* 293-312. https://doi.org/10.1016/0959-4752(94)90003-5

7 Integrating a MOOC into the postgraduate ELT curriculum: reflecting on students' beliefs with a MOOC blend

Marina Orsini-Jones[1], Barbara Conde Gafaro[2], and Shooq Altamimi[3]

Abstract

This chapter builds on the outcomes of a blended learning action-research project in its third iteration (academic year 2015-16). The FutureLearn Massive Open Online Course (MOOC) *Understanding Language: Learning and Teaching* was integrated into the curriculum of the Master of Arts (MA) in English Language Teaching (ELT) at Coventry University (UK). The MOOC was designed by the University of Southampton in collaboration with the British Council and many of its topics appeared to coincide with those on the MA in ELT module 'Theories and Methods of Language Learning and Teaching'. The initial blend trialled for the project included all students covering the same topics in various ways, e.g. in face-to-face workshops at Coventry University, on the MOOC with thousands of participants, and on the institutional virtual learning environment – Moodle – with peers on the module. This enhanced blend afforded unique opportunities for reflection on the problematic areas of knowledge encountered by students on the MA in ELT, such as learner autonomy. The work reported here was carried out by one of the authors (Altamimi), an 'expert student' who replicated the

---

1. Coventry University, Coventry, United Kingdom; m.orsini@coventry.ac.uk

2. Coventry University, Coventry, United Kingdom; condegab@uni.coventry.ac.uk

3. Ministry of Education, Isa Town, Bahrain; shoug.altamimi@windowslive.com

How to cite this chapter: Orsini-Jones, M., Conde Gafaro, B., & Altamimi, S. (2017). Integrating a MOOC into the postgraduate ELT curriculum: reflecting on students' beliefs with a MOOC blend. In Q. Kan & S. Bax (Eds), *Beyond the language classroom: researching MOOCs and other innovations* (pp. 71-83). Research-publishing.net. https://doi.org/10.14705/rpnet.2017.mooc2016.672

research design of the first cycles of the study carried out by Orsini-Jones in 2014 and 2015, and focused on learners' beliefs, rather than on learner autonomy.

Keywords: blended learning, MOOC, ELT, beliefs.

1. Introduction

This study is the third cycle of an action research project carried out in the School of Humanities at Coventry University (UK). It relates to the integration of the FutureLearn MOOC *Understanding Language: Learning and Teaching*, by the University of Southampton and the British Council, into the curriculum of the MA in ELT. The first phase of the project (semester one 2014-15) investigated the engagement of six members of staff and two expert students[4] with the blended MOOC pilot (Orsini-Jones et al., 2015) which had been integrated into the module 'Theories and Methods of Language Learning and Teaching', while the second phase (semester two 2014-15) focused on the evaluation of the students' reflection on the experience of studying the MOOC in a blended learning mode (Orsini-Jones, 2015).

The type of MOOC blend described here, where the content of a MOOC becomes an integral part of an existing curriculum in an institution that is not involved in the development of the MOOC itself, is relatively new in the UK higher education sector, but there are numerous precedents in the USA (Israel, 2013; Kim, 2015; Sandeen, 2013). Sandeen (2013) calls this type of blend a 'MOOC 3.0' or a 'distributed flip' model. The value of blending open educational resources into an existing curriculum is also supported by a study by the Higher Education Academy (HEA), as previously illustrated (Orsini-Jones, 2015, p. 5).

---

4. For further information on the concept of the 'expert student' refer to Orsini-Jones (2014).

It was hoped that the MOOC blend would offer the MA students a unique and global collaborative learning opportunity, as the FutureLearn MOOC pedagogical model is underpinned by Laurillard's (2013) education technology dialogic framework. The overall aim of this MOOC blend was to evaluate the impact of a novel blended learning experience on the MA students' perceptions and reflections regarding challenging topics in their discipline. Secondly, the study aimed at exploring how the MA students' beliefs could be affected by a multiple level meta-reflection on their knowledge and practice carried out while taking part in a relevant MOOC in blended mode.

As stated in Orsini-Jones (2015, p. 5), the MOOC was integrated into the module *Theories and Methods of Language Learning and Teaching* that carries 15 of the 180 credits on the MA in ELT. Its aim is to give students an in-depth understanding of the theories of Second Language Acquisition (SLA) and illustrate their links to approaches and methods of language teaching which they inform. The module's learning outcomes are that, on completion, students should be able to:

- critically appraise the major theories of SLA;

- discuss the relevance of SLA theories to the development of teaching approaches and methodology;

- discuss and appraise the implications of sociocultural theories for the development of second language learning and teaching approaches and methodology;

- analyse the suitability of needs of specific English language learners in specific English language learning contexts and discuss the teaching and learning approaches most appropriate to their situation.

The outcomes are summatively assessed as follows (Orsini-Jones, 2015, p. 5): one essay (at home) and a seen exam (the students receive its text a fortnight before the exam takes place). The exam comprises two questions to answer, one of which is relevant to the MOOC blend. The main topics covered by the weekly units of the MOOC were the following, and many sections coincided with an existing topic on the MA module:

- Week 1: Learning Language: Theory.

- Week 2: Language Teaching in the Classroom

- Week 3: Technology in Language Learning and Teaching: A New Environment

- Week 4: Language in Use: Global English

Orsini-Jones (2015) further points out that

> "[b]efore the integration of the MOOC into its syllabus, the module was delivered by a blend that included face-to-face contact [...] and online support provided through activities available in a dedicated Moodle website where students could access information on lectures, view relevant videos, engage in interactive tasks [and quizzes] and discuss the material covered in class in online discussion forums before, during and after the face-to-face sessions" (p. 5).

After the MOOC was introduced, the blend was enhanced by the opportunity not only to access extra online materials and new 'expert voices', but also to engage with a much wider community of practice. A MOOC navigation session was delivered face-to-face in a PC laboratory as soon as the MOOC started. At the end of each unit, the MOOC included a section called 'Reflection' where participants were expected to share the positive aspects of the week. The students on the MA were also asked to do the same on the discussion forums in Moodle.

The findings reported here stemmed from the third phase of this MOOC blend project carried out by Altamimi, an 'expert student' and one of the authors, and were reported in her MA thesis (Altamimi, 2016). Altamimi replicated the research design of the previous studies by Orsini-Jones (2015) and Orsini-Jones et al. (2015), but focused on learners' beliefs rather than learner autonomy. Also, her study did not include the intercultural learning component on *Facebook* that had characterised the second cycle of this curricular action by Orsini-Jones (2015). Altamimi explored if and how the participants' beliefs in relation to key language learning and teaching concepts had been affected by their engagement with the MOOC blend project.

2. Methodology

2.1. Context

This work is framed within the overarching transactional pedagogical enquiry approach known as 'Threshold Concepts Pedagogy' (Cousin, 2009; Flanagan, 2016), that aims to identify which of the fundamental concepts in a discipline are challenging (troublesome) for students. This is done in order to put in place ways of supporting students with crossing these curricular stumbling blocks. Threshold concepts usually present a number of troublesome areas, which are troublesome because they challenge the learner with knowledge that is 'alien' both in terms of epistemology (knowledge system/language) and ontology (learner's identity and beliefs). For example, the overarching structure of a sentence was previously identified as a threshold concept in linguistics (Orsini-Jones, 2010) and each of its components proved to be troublesome to students (e.g. morphemes, clauses, phrases).

A distinguishing feature of the threshold concepts approach discussed here is that the identification of troublesome knowledge is sought by student researchers, or 'expert students', who, having adopted threshold concepts pedagogy for their own research design, help staff members discover areas of troublesome knowledge by enabling them to approach these problematic areas from a student's perspective (Orsini-Jones, 2014). Altamimi was one of these 'expert students'. After having experienced the MOOC blend herself as a student in its second curricular cycle in 2015 (Orsini-Jones, 2015), she decided to adopt an inquiry into threshold concepts for her dissertation. She focused on a previously identified troublesome area in ELT pedagogy, i.e. teachers' beliefs (Klapper, 2006), and investigated how the MOOC blend could enable students on the September 2015 cohort of the MA in ELT to reflect on their beliefs.

MA in ELT students are not always aware of the impact that their beliefs can have on their teaching practice. This lack of awareness raises two areas of concern. The first one is that beliefs can act as a barrier or filter when these teachers (or future teachers) are attempting to further their own professional knowledge and pedagogy (Klapper, 2006). Therefore, they need to be made aware of their own beliefs and perceptions, while they are still undergoing teacher training and education, in order to explicitly develop their own pedagogical beliefs and assumptions with the underpinning of relevant research, and develop professionally as a result. The second concern is that teachers' personal learning experience is likely to influence what their teaching is going to be like (Klapper, 2006). This is not to suggest that all teaching based on personally experienced models is bad or ineffective; trainee teachers might have had positive role models who have influenced their beliefs and perceptions in a positive way. However, arbitrary and random transfer might yield problematic results when teachers adopt methods and practices unsuited to a certain group of learners or contexts (Klapper, 2006). Although it may be argued that there is no correct way to teach, teaching requires the flexibility needed to know what approach to adopt for a certain group of learners, in a specific curricular circumstance in a specific cultural setting (Kumaravadivelu, 2012). Thus, engaging in meta-reflective practices underpinned by research on language learning and teaching can be one way of achieving beneficial transfer. The research questions investigated by Altamimi were therefore the following:

- What constitutes 'troublesome knowledge' in English language learning and teaching for students on the MA in ELT?

- Would engaging with the MOOC-blend project change students' beliefs on language learning and teaching and related 'troublesome knowledge'?

Altamimi modelled her research design on previous work carried out by Orsini-Jones on the MOOC-blend on the MA in ELT (Orsini-Jones, 2015). She designed a pre-MOOC and a post-MOOC survey with the Bristol Online Survey (BOS) tool[5], but unlike Orsini-Jones (2015) who had explored learner autonomy, she focused on learners' beliefs. The BOS was selected because it allowed the gathering of a large amount of information quickly and is Data Protection Act-compliant. Both surveys consisted of mainly close-ended Likert scale questions with the inclusion of a few open-ended questions following guidelines provided by Dörnyei (2003) and were piloted by the researcher and her supervisor before being administered to the participating students. Altamimi also organised a focus group after the completion of the post-MOOC survey which enabled her to triangulate the participants' quantitative (multiple choice) and qualitative (open-ended) survey answers.

2.2. Sampling

12 self-selected students, out of the 18 who were enrolled on the MA in ELT in the 2015 September cohort, agreed to participate in the study (see Table 1 below). Participants with previous teaching experience had taught General English (GE), Academic Writing, English for Specific Purposes (ESP), English as a Second Language (ESL), English as a Foreign Language (EFL), and Literature courses.

Table 1. Demographics of pre-and post-MOOC survey sample

Participant	Mode of study	Nationality	L1	Sex	Level of Proficiency	Teaching experience	Length	Subject
1	FT	British	English	F	C2	Yes	>1	ESP
2	FT	British	English	F	C2	Yes	>1	Writing
3	FT	Norwegian	English	F	C2	No	0	
4	PT	British	English	F	C2	Yes	5	ESL/EFL
5	FT	British	English	F	C2	Yes	>1	GE

5. Available from https://research-publishing.box.com/s/fnccognqeh36gdcflw509zxdelqfv5zt

6	FT	Taiwanese	Chinese	M	B2	Yes	>1	ESL
7	FT	Chinese	Chinese	F	B2	No	0	
8	FT	Chinese	Chinese	F	B2	No	0	
9	FT	Chinese	Chinese	F	B2	No	0	
10	FT	Chinese	Chinese	F	C1	No	0	
11	FT	Nigerian	Yoruba	F	C1	Yes	1	Literature
12	FT	Indonesian	Bahasa	F	C1	No	0	

3. Results and discussion

3.1. General perceptions

Regarding the blended aspect of the project, in the focus group participants agreed that, in line with previous results (Orsini-Jones, 2015), the MOOC was a useful open educational addition to an existing module. They stated that they had enjoyed the flexibility in the access to extra materials afforded by the MOOC, and they were particularly complimentary of how it supplemented the module in various ways, including extra references that they could use in their coursework, and providing summaries of topics discussed on the module in class.

The fact that the blend was perceived as a positive addition to their curriculum was also reinforced by the answers to the relevant questions in the post-MOOC BOS. Table 2 below illustrates a noticeable shift in beliefs on online learning in the 'agree' column, even if there is a small increase in the 'disagree' percentage in the first question reported.

Table 2.   Attitudes towards online learning in the pre- and post-MOOC surveys

Learning a language online can motivate learners.			
Time	Agree	Neutral	Disagree
Pre	58%	34%	8%
Post	75%	8%	17%
Learning about language learning online can motivate teachers.			
Time	Agree	Neutral	Disagree
Pre	42%	33%	25%
Post	75%	8%	17%

While participants were on the whole positive about the MOOC blend experience, they found the MOOC discussions after each topic difficult to navigate, due to the number of postings. This might call for better scaffolding in Bruner's (1983) terms of the dialogic aspect of the MOOC.

3.2. Grammar and CLIL

Another interesting outcome was that while grammar awareness was believed to be particularly challenging by seven of the 12 respondents in the pre-MOOC survey, in the post-MOOC survey, grammar did not emerge as a particularly troublesome area. The seven participants were therefore asked to elaborate on the change in relation to their grammar beliefs in the focus group discussion. They stated that they viewed grammar as less problematic after having engaged with the MOOC and having explored grammar issues on the relevant modules with their tutors. On the other hand, they stated that Content and Language Integrated Learning (CLIL) was difficult to understand and challenging to implement. This perception had been reinforced by watching and discussing the videos of the two sample CLIL classes in the second week of the MOOC. The perceived challenge in the understanding of CLIL could possibly relate to the fact that the topic was included in the assessed test and that the sample CLIL video illustrations in the MOOC did not appear to propose effective CLIL models.

3.3. Autonomy

The focus group discussion confirmed that autonomy (as defined by Benson, 2001) is a troublesome concept. It appeared to be alien in terms of ontology (a concept that is alien to the identity of the learner), as previously discussed by Orsini-Jones (2015). The challenge to the identity of the learner posed by the concept of autonomy can result in MA students developing a resistance to it, not necessarily because the concept is difficult to understand, but because they do not believe in it. British and non-British participants mentioned different reasons behind their resistance to the implementation of autonomy in their teaching practice. Non-British participants emphasised cultural differences between what they had learned on the module, the MOOC, and their own local context as shown below:

> "My experience was a little different [to that of British participants]. It's because of cultural differences. My context in Taiwan – frankly speaking, I don't want to try autonomy, to try that stuff... I think the learner over there – sometimes if the teacher doesn't push them they don't care. They tend to not do the extra reading, they tend to not do self-studying. So if, like, I ask them to go online and check MOOC... I think they won't do it" (Focus Group transcription, Participant E, 3rd December 2015).

It is interesting to see the word 'stuff' used for autonomy with a tinge of derogatory connotation in the quote above, to signal conceptual distance from it.

The British participants, on the other hand, emphasised how pressure from the educational establishment where they were based could work against the adoption of autonomy. Participant D, who was the most experienced teacher in the sample, mentioned that 'schemes of work' in the British system were not conducive to the development of autonomy in learners (and teachers). However, she stated that the MOOC blend project had given her some ideas:

> "I've learned a couple of really good ways of making my learners take control of their learning rather than me giving a lot of structure. I'm trying to take more of a "guide on the side" approach.... at the very start I will be asking them [my learners] what sort of writing they're struggling with, and I'll select some activities for them according to their level, but I'll let them select some activities for them[selves] as well" (Participant D, focus group transcription, 3rd December 2015).

The extract demonstrates that Participant D understood that teachers would still have a role in an autonomous classroom, but that the nature of their role would be different: rather than them 'dictating' all classroom procedures and activities, they would give their students some choice and guide them through their learning journey. On the other hand, MA students who had no teaching experience viewed an autonomous classroom as one that would not have enough teacher involvement, and be full of chaos.

4. Conclusion

Concluding remarks are reported here with reference to each one of the initial research questions posed in the methodology section.

- What constitutes 'troublesome knowledge' in English language learning and teaching for students on the MA in ELT?

Some troublesome areas of knowledge identified by the MA students were similar to the ones identified in previous related literature, i.e. grammar (Orsini-Jones, 2010). However, CLIL emerged as a new troublesome one. This was an unexpected outcome that will require further investigation and validation with a bigger sample of participants.

- Would engaging with the MOOC-blend project change the MA students' beliefs on language learning and teaching and related troublesome knowledge?

The pre- and post-MOOC surveys revealed that engaging with the MOOC appeared to have changed students' beliefs regarding some areas of troublesome knowledge (like grammar) but did not appear to have clarified the majority of the participants' beliefs on autonomy. Many appeared to associate it only with independent learning, rather than seeing its links with reflection and collaboration highlighted by Little (2001, p. 31). Also, through the tracking of individual responses to the pre- and post-MOOC survey answers and their triangulation with the focus group discussion, it appeared that participants had exaggerated the changes to their beliefs. Factors that might have contributed towards this may be related to the survey's 'halo effect' (Dörnyei, 2003) and participants' impressions being provided upon initial limited interaction with the MOOC, hence not going beyond the technology's 'wow factor' (Murray & Barnes, 1998).

However, the results illustrated that engaging with the MOOC transformed some of the beliefs on online learning held by the students on the MA in ELT. Furthermore, the majority of the participants recommended that MOOCs should be integrated into more modules. The authors of this study are investigating how such a blend can impact on the training of teachers in different countries on a much larger scale (in the UK, the Netherlands, and China) through a British Council funded project, B-MELTT: Blending MOOCs into English Language Teacher Training. A limitation of the study reported here was the number of participants involved. As B-MELTT has over 130 participants, it is hoped that its results will make the generalisation of the outcomes of this small scale study more valid.

References

Altamimi, S. (2016). *An investigation into teachers' beliefs regarding troublesome knowledge in language learning and teaching in the context of studying on a related MOOC.* Unpublished Master's thesis. Coventry University, Coventry, England.

Benson, P. (2001). *Teaching and researching: autonomy in language learning.* Harlow, England: Pearson Education Limited.

Bruner, J. S. (1983). *Child's talk: learning to use language.* London, England: WW Norton.

Cousin, G. (2009). *Researching learning in higher education: an introduction to contemporary methods and approaches.* London, England: Routledge.

Dörnyei, Z. (2003). *Questionnaires in second language research: construction, administration, and processing.* London, England: Routledge.

Flanagan, M. (2016, November 22). *Threshold concepts: undergraduate teaching, postgraduate training and professional development - a short introduction and bibliography.* http://www.ee.ucl.ac.uk/~mflanaga/thresholds.html

Israel, M. J. (2013). Effectiveness of integrating MOOCs in traditional classrooms for undergraduate students. *IRRODL-The International Review of Open and Distributed Learning, 16*(5), 102-118. https://doi.org/10.19173/irrodl.v16i5.2222

Kim, P. (Ed.). (2015). *Massive open online courses: the MOOC revolution*. Abingdon, England: Routledge.

Klapper, J. (2006). *Understanding and developing good practice: language teaching in higher education*. London, England: CILT, The National Centre for Languages.

Kumaravadivelu, B. (2012). *Language teacher education for a global society: a modular model for knowing, analyzing, recognizing, doing, and seeing*. New York, NY: Routledge.

Laurillard, D. (2013). *Rethinking university teaching: a conversational framework for the effective use of learning technologies*. Abingdon, England: Routledge.

Little, D. (2001). Learner autonomy and the challenge of tandem language learning via the Internet. In A. Chambers & G. Davies (Eds), *ICT and language learning: a European perspective* (pp. 29-38). Abingdon, London: Swets & Zeitlinger Publishers.

Murray, L., & Barnes, A. (1998). Beyond the "Wow" factor- evaluating multimedia language learning software from a pedagogical viewpoint. *System, 26(2)*, 249-59.

Orsini-Jones, M. (2010). Troublesome grammar knowledge and action research-led assessment design: learning from liminality. In R. Land, J. H. Meyer, & C. Baillie (Eds), *Threshold concepts and transformational learning* (pp. 281-299). Rotterdam, Netherlands: Sense.

Orsini-Jones, M. (2014). Towards a role-reversal model of threshold concept pedagogy. In C. O'Mahony, A. Buchanan, M. O'Rourke, & B. Higgs (Eds), *Proceedings of the National Academy for Integration of Research, Teaching and Learning's Sixth Annual Conference and the Fourth Biennial Threshold Concepts Conference [E-publication], Threshold concepts: From personal practice to communities of practice* (pp. 78-82). Trinity College, Dublin: NAIRTL. http://www.nairtl.ie/documents/EPub_2012Proceedings.pdf#page=88

Orsini-Jones, M. (2015). *Innovative pedagogies series: integrating a MOOC into the MA in English language teaching at Coventry University: innovation in blended learning practice*. https://www.heacademy.ac.uk/system/files/marina_orsini_jones_final_1.pdf

Orsini-Jones, M., Pibworth-Dolinski, L., Cribb, M., Brick, B., Gazeley-Eke, Z., Leinster, H., & Lloyd, E. (2015). Learning about language learning on a MOOC: how massive, open, online and "course"? In F. Helm, L. Bradley, M. Guarda, & S. Thouësny (Eds), *Critical CALL – Proceedings of the 2015 EUROCALL Conference, Padova, Italy* (pp. 450-457). Dublin, Ireland: Research-publishing.net. https://doi.org/10.14705/rpnet.2015.000374

Sandeen, C. (2013). Integrating MOOCs into traditional higher education: the emerging "MOOC 3.0" era. *Change, 45(6)*, 34-39. https://doi.org/10.1080/00091383.2013.842103

8. MOOCs for language learning – opportunities and challenges: the case of the Open University Italian Beginners' MOOCs

Anna Motzo[1] and Anna Proudfoot[2]

Abstract

Massive Open Online Courses (MOOCs) are a fairly recent development in online education. Language MOOCs (LMOOCs) have recently been added to the ever-growing list of open courses offered by various providers, including FutureLearn. For learners, MOOCs offer an innovative and inexpensive alternative to formal and traditional learning. For course designers and developers, this emerging learning model raises important issues concerning the affordances of the new learning environment and the rationale for adopting a particular pedagogical approach to sustain the learning experience. The authors offer an insight into their own experiences in designing and delivering an Italian for Beginners MOOC on FutureLearn. This case study explores the opportunities and challenges we met and the link with existing research.

Keywords: massive open online courses, MOOC, formal learning, informal learning, online language learning.

---

1. The Open University, Milton Keynes, United Kingdom; a.motzo@open.ac.uk

2. The Open University, Milton Keynes, United Kingdom; anna.proudfoot@open.ac.uk

How to cite this chapter: Motzo, A., & Proudfoot, A. (2017). MOOCs for language learning – opportunities and challenges: the case of the Open University Italian Beginners' MOOCs. In Q. Kan & S. Bax (Eds), *Beyond the language classroom: researching MOOCs and other innovations* (pp. 85-97). Research-publishing.net. https://doi.org/10.14705/rpnet.2017.mooc2016.673

Chapter 8

1. Introduction and context

In recent years, the number of educational resources freely available online has increased exponentially thanks to the development of the Open Educational Resources (OERs) movement and the provision of MOOCs (McGreal, 2013). OERs display various characteristics; openness, free access, and use and re-purposing of the resources, all common principles which promote "the building of ubiquitous learning networks as well as reducing the knowledge divide that separates and partitions societies" (McGreal, 2013, p. xviii).

MOOCs represent the principle of supporting openness in education while at the same time embracing technological innovation. Run entirely online, MOOCs are a development of distance learning which followed on naturally from the rise of online education and the development of open access universities around the world (Siemens, 2013).

Arguably, the first MOOC was created and delivered by George Siemens and Stephen Downes in 2008 (mentioned in Parr, 2013) to test out connectivism, the learning theory they developed which posits that learners work together to co-construct and distribute knowledge through networks, as practitioners in a community. Since then, the interest in this new way of learning and teaching has constantly increased to the point that 2012 was described in the New York Times as "the year of the MOOC" (Pappano, 2012, cited in Siemens, 2013, p. 5).

The Open University UK (henceforth OU), launched in the late 1960's and as one of the major exponents of distance learning, started to engage with the MOOC landscape with the openED 2.0, a European MOOC on business and management. By 2012, the OU was running its own MOOCs, for example the Open Translation MOOC, while was also setting up the FutureLearn MOOC platform in partnership with 11 higher education institutions. Fully owned by the OU, FutureLearn was the first UK-led MOOC learning platform, its first MOOC running in September 2013. In terms of languages, the OU School of Languages and Applied Linguistics launched their first language MOOC (a programme of six Spanish for Beginners courses) in August 2016, followed by a programme of six Italian for Beginners courses in September 2016.

2. Current literature on MOOCs and LMOOCs

The main principles of MOOCs are autonomy, diversity, openness and interactivity (Downes, 2012); socio-constructivism, collaborative learning and connectivism are the theoretical principles that underpin the development of MOOCs, whereby self-directed learners support the learning community through social interaction and active engagement in the learning process. However, there are different approaches to MOOC design and delivery deriving from distinctive theoretical principles as well as from subject-specific considerations. Since the terms were first coined by Downes in 2012, the main dichotomy has been between cMOOCs and xMOOCs.

The former follows a connectivist approach, which posits that "knowledge is distributed across a network of connections, and that accordingly learning consists of the ability to construct and traverse those networks" (Downes, 2012, p. 9). In connectivist MOOCs, course content is not viewed and presented as the object of learning in itself but rather as an instrument that stimulates learning and that activates learner engagement within a 'community of practitioners'. In this model, which emphasises simultaneously open social learning and learner autonomy, learners help each other to aggregate and distribute knowledge through various networks, while educators demonstrate tactics and techniques and model the "approach, language and world view of a successful practitioner" (Downes, 2011, n.p.).

xMOOCs, on the other hand, offer a wider audience a taster for high-quality university courses. They are built in structured content and follow an instructivist approach whereby courses are designed with specific learning goals in mind and teaching is fundamentally embedded in the web course resources (Ferguson, Coughlan, & Heredotou, 2016). In xMOOCs, the team of educators is normally responsible for course delivery as well as for its design. As indicated by Littlejohn (2013), such MOOCs do not normally require a high level of interaction amongst the learners. The majority of these types of MOOCs, rather than following a connectivist framework, use a more traditional and instructivist pedagogical approach (Kennedy, 2014; Staubitz et al., 2015) which focuses on theories of learner autonomy and self-regulation rather than on social learning.

LMOOCs are an emerging category. Bàrcena Read, Martín-Monje, and Castrillo (2014) is arguably the first major contribution to an analysis of theoretical as well as methodological issues related to LMOOCs, which the authors define as "dedicated web-based online courses for second languages with unrestricted access and potentially unlimited participation" (p .1). The authors also point out that one of the main challenges faced by LMOOCs is that learning a language is fundamentally skill-based rather than knowledge-based, and practising the skill requires learning with others, while the majority of existing LMOOCs follow an instructivist approach which does not necessarily promote collaboration. The challenge and also opportunity for LMOOC educators is therefore to foster an environment which enhances social learning by including a range of activities and tools which stimulate discussion and collaboration amongst participants.

Moreira Teixeira and Mota (2014) argue that in the current xMOOC model, the tools allowing full collaboration are limited (e.g. the discussion tool) and that the xMOOCs do not make the most of the tools (i.e. social networks) used by the cMOOC. They suggest a new pedagogical approach for LMOOCs which they call iMOOC, and which they introduced at the Open University of Portugal. The iMOOC is based on a synthesis of cMOOC and xMOOC, and draws on the potential of the networked approach as well as the structured Higher Education pedagogy. The 'i' represents individual responsibility, interaction, interpersonal relationships, innovation, and inclusion. Students use their own Personal Learning Environment (PLE) to manage their learning and engage in conversation with other learners.

Conversely, Ferguson et al. (2016), in their report on OU MOOCs, indicate that MOOCs hosted by the UK-based platform FutureLearn are underpinned by the pedagogy of conversational learning with a learning environment that fosters social interaction and collaboration between learners mainly through the use of embedded tools such as discussions. It is argued that by shifting from an instructivist to a more socio-constructivist learning environment, more opportunities and challenges arise for the language course designer.

In this case study, we therefore discuss the challenges and opportunities we faced in designing and delivering our Italian for Beginners MOOCs on the FutureLearn platform and how they relate to these various existing approaches to MOOCs, and language MOOCs in particular.

3. The OU Italian for Beginners' MOOCs

The Italian for Beginners MOOCs – as with the other MOOCs hosted by FutureLearn – are designed on socio-constructivist principles and follow the xMOOC model outlined above, where teaching is embedded in and constitutes an integral part of the course design to allow learners to progress autonomously and independently. Learning in this case is facilitated by a well-structured and organised presentation of the learning resources and activities designed to achieve specific outcomes. The MOOC is learner-centred, provides a high degree of flexibility, and in contrast to other xMOOCs that do not support collaborative learning (Staubitz et al., 2015), it seeks to encourage interaction through the discussion areas, where collaborative learning can take place using dialogue, peer exchange and feedback, as well as guidance from course organisers.

Each of the six MOOCs in the Italian for Beginners programme lasts for four weeks and each week has up to 23 activities called 'steps'. There are a variety of activities such as quizzes, articles and discussions. Activities are designed to encourage use of the target language. Discussions follow many of the activities, providing learners with an opportunity to consolidate or reflect on their learning. Discussions are embedded in the learning content and can be divided into two main types: those which require learners to write and post something in Italian, and those which ask learners to reflect or comment on an aspect of culture and society, perhaps making a comparison with the same aspect in their own country of origin or of residence. Students have the opportunity to take a progress test at the end of each week where general feedback is provided and a score given.

In the OU language MOOCs, the content is semi-structured; while still allowing flexibility in the way learners engage with the material, it follows a clear progression from the simplest to the most complex steps. However, since learners navigate the site autonomously, they can complete the activities in any order, thereby organising their own learning according to their interests, abilities, needs, etc.

The interactive activities elicit the four skills. Reading and listening skills are developed and practised through comprehension activities, while learners can practise writing and speaking skills through productive activities. Learners can record their spoken contributions using any commercially available software and are encouraged to post their written or recorded contributions on the discussion page.

As already mentioned, the main collaborative feature offered by the FutureLearn platform is a Discussion tool. Through the discussion facility, learners can connect with each other, share knowledge and collaborate. In the Italian for Beginners course, the collaborative practices afforded by the discussion tool enhance peer learning and support and offer activities which foster the sharing of knowledge.

Collaborative practices are designed to help build a sense of community. Each discussion is triggered by an activity or article written by the academic team. These can be used to stimulate language practice using the target language or develop intercultural awareness through comparison and reflection. Examples of the two activities are shown in Figure 1 and Figure 2.

In this first example (Figure 1), the participants use the target language to have simple meaningful conversations with – and to receive feedback from – both fellow participants and the academic team. In this way, learners practise their language working together with others and this constitutes the basis for the formation of an online community. In practice, the number of comments tended to peak after topics which allowed learners to exchange information about their own lives, e.g. mealtimes, their family, their workplace, etc.

Figure 1. Example of language exchange in Italian

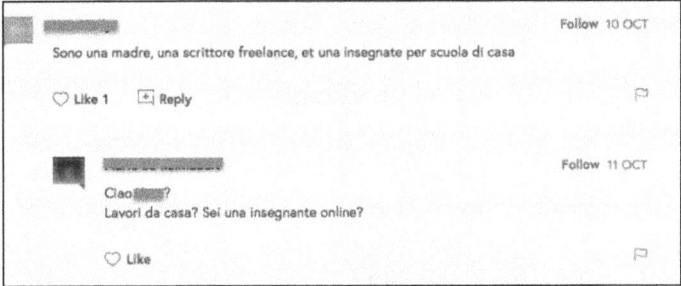

Figure 2. Sample of a discussion on a linguistic-cultural issue: 'Nouns denoting professions traditionally dominated by men'

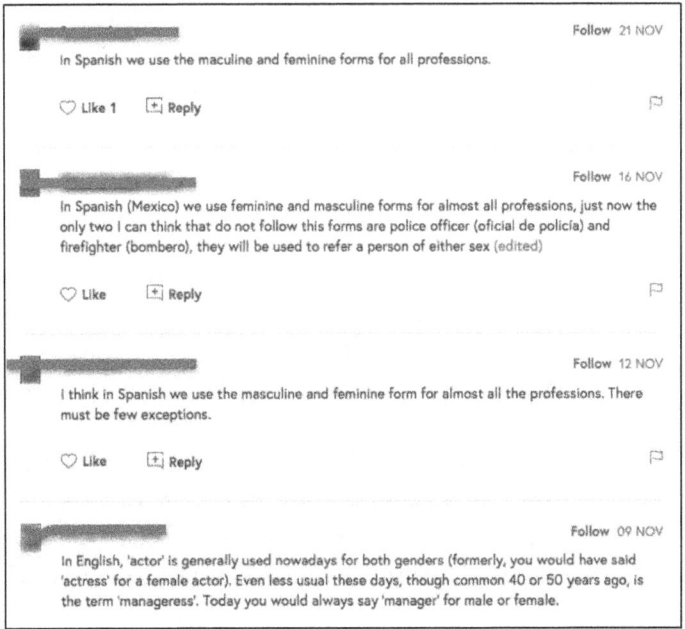

The discussion tool is also used to stimulate conversation around topics concerning Italian culture, language and society, which provide participants with the opportunity to exchange knowledge and discuss the differences with their own language and culture. As evidenced in Figure 2, this use of discussion allows participants to interact with each other openly and expand their learning beyond the subject matter (Italian). The discussion also encourages intercultural awareness.

As shown in Figure 3, threads where learners could exchange information about their own life (such as where they worked or describing a friend) attracted a high number of comments. The thread on 'Nouns denoting professions traditionally dominated by men', in line with other similar threads on linguistic-cultural issues, also attracted a relatively high number of responses (571), in comparison to threads focusing on purely linguistic aspects, such as pronunciation or verbs. This suggests that both relevant topical threads and linguistic-cultural threads lend themselves more naturally to social learning practices such as knowledge sharing. The role played by the discussion tool, therefore, echoes some of the elements outlined by Downes (2012) in his connectivist theory in that learners support each other, perceive the benefits of learning together and feel part of a community. However, it is also interesting to note that during these interactions learners only rarely address each other directly. We argue that this might be related to the sense of anonymity felt by learners in such a massive learning environment.

The role played by the community of learners is crucial in a massive course where moderation, support and feedback represent a big challenge for the lead educators. At the same time, learners come with diverse expertise and knowledge which may be extremely valuable within the community. Therefore, in order to encourage collaborative practice and maximise peer learning support, we used a number of features such as 'rating' and 'following' participants. We used the system of 'likes' to reward learners who either provided feedback to others, commenting on their written contributions to discussions, or were simply quite active participants. This included native speakers of Italian who voluntarily provided corrections and feedback to their peers. The reinforcement and approval of active participants proved to be a fairly successful way to maintain their engagement. Furthermore, since the massive number of participants made it practically impossible to read all comments and postings, we also relied on identifying and consequently 'following' the more active learners. Obviously, learners too can autonomously use this facility to connect with other learners, and in such a way are a variety of networks formed within the community.

Figure 3.   Visual representation of learners' participation in each discussion thread

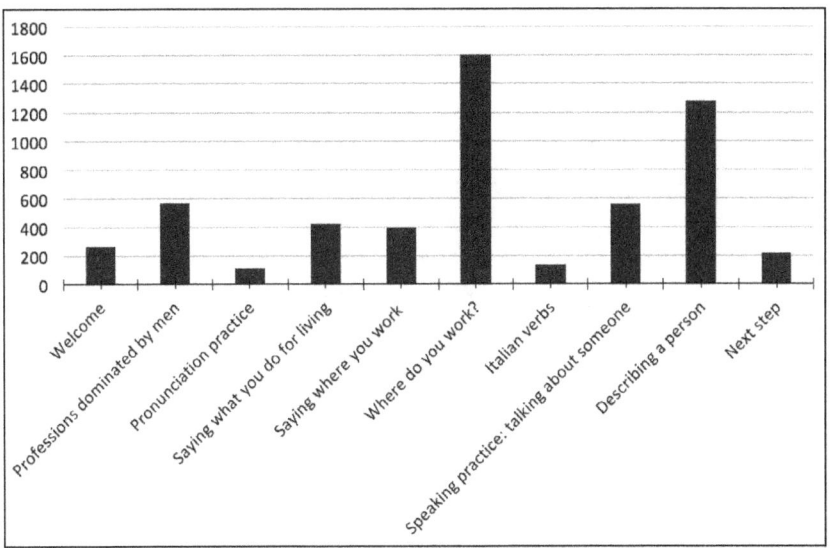

4.   Discussion

Developing an LMOOC presents a number of opportunities and challenges. Here we attempt to address just a few.

4.1. Approach and principles

Although there are various examples of OU MOOCs designed using a connectivist approach – one example is the Open Translation MOOC (Beaven et al., 2013) – the FutureLearn language MOOCs follow a broadly xMOOC model. For most universities developing and delivering MOOCs, in fact, the xMOOC model is generally preferred, since it gives them the opportunity to repurpose course content. It allows universities to innovate, while not changing their culture or pedagogical approach (Moreira Teixeira & Mota, 2014). This is in fact the strategy followed in the development of the OU's Italian for Beginners courses on FutureLearn, which were based on the first six units of the OU's Italian for Beginners module.

By using the affordances offered by the FutureLearn platform, however, we were able to encourage collaborative practice, for example through the use of the discussion tool, thus replicating elements of the collaborative learning of the cMOOCs. From a preliminary evaluation of the first run of the programme, we feel that the level of participation in these discussions was good (see Figure 3 above) but could be further improved, possibly by rethinking task design to give more weight to contributing. This could be achieved by embedding in the discussion activities and fostering collaboration amongst the learners, who could perhaps organise themselves in small online working groups in order to complete specific tasks.

4.2. Moderation

For the course team, a significant challenge is that of moderating discussions and responding to queries, as the number of participants is exceedingly high: in Week 1 of MOOC1 alone, for instance, there were in total 30,956 comments. The FutureLearn platform does not allow advanced sorting by keyword, making it difficult to filter comments, even within a discussion page, but does allow users to sort by contributor, for example selecting only comments by the educator(s) or by those contributors they are 'following'. It also allows sorting by 'Likes' so that the highest rated comments can be located easily.

4.3. Cultural issues

The heterogeneous composition of the participants – who can come from countries as far apart as Mexico and Kazakhstan – can present both opportunities and challenges in terms of their different backgrounds and past learning experiences. Working across boundaries, whether geographical, political, religious or cultural, requires a certain level of intercultural awareness in learners and moderators and increased sensitivity relating to socio-cultural issues. An article about the family in Italy which included references to civil partnerships led to some polemical comments in the Discussion area.

4.4. Retention

Common to all MOOCs is the low number of learners who complete or who participate fully. Jordan (2015) found median completion rates of around 12%. There may be multiple reasons why this occurs. Firstly, there is a high percentage of leisure learners, who neither need nor want a Certificate of Completion or similar document. Secondly, the courses are free, so there is no financial commitment involved. More research would need to be done to establish whether completion rates are lower on xMOOCs than on cMOOCs where learners establish learning communities from the outset. If this is the case, then incorporating more of the elements or characteristics of cMOOCs might provide a solution. For instance, in LMOOCs, learners could be encouraged to use social networks and to set up small groups for speaking practice on Skype or Facetime. By adopting a learning management system which would allow us to embed other media and resources as part of students' PLE, as suggested by Moreira Teixeira and Mota (2014), the learning experience could be enriched.

5. Conclusion

In this paper we have presented the opportunities and challenges for course teams presented by this emerging learning environment, using as a case study the OU's Italian for Beginners MOOC hosted by FutureLearn.

MOOCs can potentially play an important role in bridging the gap between formal and informal learning and in widening participation. They fulfil the brief of making educational resources freely available to a wider audience, and they foster innovation in pedagogic approaches, allowing universities to test new ways of delivering courses. However, for course designers and leaders, they also present challenges in managing the learning process, mainly due to their massive scale. This is particularly true for language MOOCs which are built around skills, not content, and where interaction between learners is perhaps more important.

The limitations of the xMOOC model have been discussed above and solutions suggested. Further research is needed to gain an insight into the learner experience and to gather data about participation and completion. As MOOCs evolve further, and platforms become more sophisticated, the nature of the learning experience will inevitably change and universities and other providers need to change with it.

References

Bárcena, E., Read, T., Martín-Monje, E., & Castrillo, M. D. (2014). Analysing student participation in foreign language MOOCs: a case study. *EMOOCs 2014: European MOOCs Stakeholders Summit* (pp. 11-17).

Beaven, T., Comas-Quinn, A., Hauck, M., de los Arcos, B., & Lewis, T. (2013). The open translation MOOC: creating online communities to transcend linguistic barriers. *In OER 13 Creating a virtuous circle, Nottingham.*

Downes, S. (2011, May 25). The role of the educator. *The Huffington Post.* http://www.huffingtonpost.com/stephen-downes/the-role-of-the-educator_b_790937.html

Downes, S. (2012). *Connectivism and connective knowledge: Essays on meaning and learning networks.* Stephen Downes Web. http://www.downes.ca/files/Connective_Knowledge-19May2012.pdf

Downes, S. (2012). Massively open online courses are 'here to stay'. *Stephen Downes.* http://www.downes.ca/post/58676

Ferguson, R., Coughlan, T., & Heredotou C. (2016). *MOOCs: what the Open University research tells us*. The Open University, Milton Keynes: Institute of Educational Technology.

Jordan, K. (2015). Massive open online course completion rates revisited: assessment, length and attrition. *International Review of Research in Open and Distributed Learning, 16*(3, 341–358. http://oro.open.ac.uk/43566/

Kennedy, J. (2014). Characteristics of massive open online courses (MOOCs): a research review, 2009-2012. *Journal of Interactive Online Learning, 13*(1).

Littlejohn, A. (2013). *Understanding massive open online courses*. New Delhi: CEMCA.

McGreal, R. (2013). Introduction: the need for open educational resources. In R. McGreal, W. Kinuthia, & S. Marshall (Eds), *Open educational resources: innovation, research and practice*. Commonwealth of Learning, Athabasca University.

Moreira Teixeira, A., & Mota, J. (2014). A proposal for the methodological design of collaborative language MOOCs. In E. Martin-Monje & E. Bárcena (Eds), *Language MOOCs: providing learning, transcending boundaries*. De Gruyter Open.

Pappano, L. (2012, November 2). The year of the MOOC. *The New York Times*. http://www.edinaschools.org/cms/lib07/MN01909547/Centricity/Domain/272/The%20Year%20of%20the%20MOOC%20NY%20Times.pdf

Parr, C. (2013, October 17). MOOC creators criticise courses' lack of creativity. *Times Higher Education*. https://www.timeshighereducation.com/news/mooc-creators-criticise-courses-lack-of-creativity/2008180.article

Siemens, G. (2013). Massive open online courses: innovation in education? In R. McGreal, W. Kinuthia, & S. Marshall (Eds), *Open educational resources: innovation, research and practice* (pp. 5-16). Commonwealth of Learning, Athabasca University.

Staubitz, T., Pfeiffer, T., Renz, J., Willems, C., & Meinel, C. (2015). Collaborative learning. In *ICERI2015 8th annual International Conference of Education, Research and Innovation, Seville, Spain* (pp. 18-20).

9. An exploration of the use of mobile applications to support the learning of Chinese characters employed by students of Chinese as a foreign language

Amanda Mason[1] and Zhang Wenxin[2]

Abstract

At present, there are few studies which explore the learning strategies employed by students of Chinese as a Foreign Language (CFL) and even fewer that focus specifically on mobile application use. This study provides insights into how adult learners at varying levels of proficiency employ mobile apps to support their Chinese character learning. Data were collected from a survey completed by 140 learners and semi-structured interviews with eight subjects. The findings demonstrate that most of the participants are using mobile apps to support their character learning. The most widely used mobile app is Pleco, but only a small proportion of its functionality is exploited. The most frequently used app-based strategies include looking up example sentences that contain new words and viewing stroke orders. The study suggests that students recognise the value of mobile apps in their learning but may need training in how to exploit their full potential.

Keywords: Chinese character learning, vocabulary learning strategies, mobile applications, Chinese as a foreign language.

---

1. Liverpool John Moores University, Liverpool, United Kingdom; a.mason@ljmu.ac.uk

2. Elite Technology and Education Ltd, Liverpool, United Kingdom; w.zhang@elitete.co.uk

How to cite this chapter: Mason, A., & Zhang, W. (2017). An exploration of the use of mobile applications to support the learning of Chinese characters employed by students of Chinese as a foreign language. In Q. Kan & S. Bax (Eds), *Beyond the language classroom: researching MOOCs and other innovations* (pp. 99-112). Research-publishing.net. https://doi.org/10.14705/rpnet.2017.mooc2016.674

Chapter 9

1. Introduction

With the rise of the Chinese economy and China's increasing political and cultural influence, there has been a growing interest in learning CFL. The value of learning Chinese and its culture is now recognised by organisations such as the British Council in the UK (British Council, 2013), and this is demonstrated by the sharp increase in the number of CFL learners over the last ten years (Hanban, 2013).

1.1. The challenges for learners of CFL

Learning to read and write is usually perceived as the most challenging aspect of learning CFL, particularly for those students whose first language has an alphabetic system (Hu, 2010). Chinese has a logographic writing system in which each symbol (character) represents an idea and has little correspondence to its pronunciation (Sung & Wu, 2011). To be able to read a newspaper in Chinese, it is estimated that one needs to be able to recognise approximately 3,000 characters (Sung, 2012) which presents an enormous challenge to CFL learners. As Sung and Wu (2011) point out, becoming fully literate in Chinese, that is, knowing how to pronounce, recognise, produce, and understand the meanings of commonly used characters, requires a considerable amount of effort for CFL learners whose first language has an alphabetic system. Thus, most learners spend much of their study time focusing on character learning, and as the character is the basic unit of vocabulary, this can be classified as vocabulary learning.

1.2. Second language vocabulary learning strategy research

Learners' use of Language Learning Strategies (LLSs) has long been recognised as significant in understanding the relative success of language learners (Oxford, 1990), and the findings of research in this area have guided language educators in helping learners become more effective. Schmitt (1997), building on this work and his own research on vocabulary learning and teaching, developed a taxonomy of Vocabulary Learning Strategies (VLSs). However, this taxonomy, like Oxford's (1990), is based mainly on research of learners of English as a second language. It therefore reflects both the alphabetic writing system of English and English morphology, and as such, is limited in its transferability to the CFL context. Similarly, much of the research investigating LLSs and VLSs may not be relevant for CFL teachers and learners due to the nature of the Chinese writing system, mentioned in the following section. For example, learning a new word in Chinese involves knowing the shape and stroke order of the character(s), and knowing the pronunciation, including the tone.

1.3. Research on CFL learner strategies

The increase in CFL teaching and learning has led to a recognition of this gap and studies have begun to appear which have explored strategy use by CFL learners. Two of the earliest studies were conducted in the US University context (Shen, 2005; Wang, 1998) and a more recent study has been conducted with adolescent learners in a UK secondary school (Grenfell & Harris, 2015). The findings of all these studies seem to suggest that most learners rely heavily on mechanical repetition strategies such as writing out characters repeatedly with the correct stroke order and self-testing by writing out characters from memory (Shen, 2005; Wang, 1998). As Grenfell and Harris (2015) point out, the effort in doing this can "leave little cognitive space for the deployment of time-consuming but higher level strategies" (p. 1) such as association, where learners try to make connections with previously learned words (Schmitt, 1997).

1.4. Mobile apps and VLSs

Given the challenges of character learning, more research is needed into what strategies might help learners become more efficient. In their review of research on second language learners' vocabulary strategies, Nyikos and Macaro (2007) note that the only real advantage of electronic dictionaries over conventional dictionaries is speed and efficiency, but for most CFL learners, this is a major understatement; electronic dictionaries with handwriting input tools significantly reduce the time it takes to look up an unknown character compared with the conventional approach. A study by Levy and Steel (2015) of language learners in an Australian university found that electronic dictionary use plays a very important role for learners' daily learning. As Godwin-Jones (2011) notes, such dictionaries and other language learning tools are now widely available as apps on mobile devices. For CFL learners, mobile apps may not only increase efficiency in learning, but may also provide more opportunities for engagement with the target language, particularly in regular short study bursts and during "dead time" (Rosell-Aguilar & Kan, 2015, p. 29). Although there has been a proliferation of research on Mobile Assisted Language Learning (MALL) over the last two decades (Burston, 2015), there have been relatively few studies of apps to support CFL learning. This paper therefore attempts to address this gap by attempting to answer the following research questions:

- What mobile apps are used by CFL learners to learn Chinese characters?

- How do CFL learners use mobile apps to learn Chinese characters?

The findings reported in this paper are part of a larger study into strategy use in general for character learning and how that might change with experience and proficiency.

2. Methodology

To explore both the use of learning strategies and mobile applications, the study adopted a mixed-methods research design. Quantitative data were collected via a survey and then qualitative data were collected through interviews with CFL learners. The questionnaire was designed to identify the apps most commonly used by learners to support their character learning strategies. The interviews were designed to gain a more detailed picture of how learners made use of apps in their learning context. Both the survey and interviews were conducted in English.

As the study was exploratory in nature with the aim of gaining initial insights into learners' usage of mobile apps, a convenience sampling strategy was adopted for the survey. The authors used their networks to identify CFL learners to take part in the interviews. Care was taken to achieve a sample which included students with a range of proficiency levels and different types of learning experience.

The questionnaire was divided into two main sections: the first section aimed to collect background information such as learner proficiency and experience; the second focused on learners' use of apps for character learning. Students were asked to select all the character learning strategies they employed with apps from a list of ten provided (shown in Table 1), and to indicate which app(s) were used for a specific strategy. Six of these items were based on Shen's (2005) strategy inventory, and a further four strategies were added based on the authors' knowledge and experience of commonly used apps.

Xi'an Jiaotong University in China has a School of International Education with more than 800 CFL learners. With the assistance of the authors' professional contacts, CFL students at this School were invited to participate in the survey. Hard copies of the questionnaire were distributed to CFL learners with a range of proficiency levels. The completed questionnaires were scanned and returned by the contact via e-mail. A total of 132 completed questionnaires were returned. In addition, a further eight surveys were completed by students who had also agreed to participate in the interviews (as described below). The data was coded, input into Excel, and analysed. The survey respondents were classified into three proficiency levels: beginners (CEFR[3] A1-A2) (35%, N=49), intermediate (CEFR B1-B2) (42%, N=52), and advanced (CEFR C1 to C2) (23%, N=32). This was based on the approximate number of characters that respondents reported being able to recognise, which was then linked to the Hanyu Shuiping Kaoshi (HSK) Chinese proficiency examination and the current Hanban (2014) benchmarks with the CEFR.

Invitations to take part in the interviews were e-mailed to authors' professional contacts who had studied or were currently studying Chinese. The e-mail

---

3. Common European Framework of Reference for languages

contained information about the purpose of the research and what it would entail. Those who agreed to take part were asked to sign a consent form giving their permission for the interview to be recorded.

Between May 2016 and October 2016, eight interviews were conducted either face-to-face or online via Skype and recorded using a digital voice recorder. The interviewees were asked to share their learning experience in general, describe their overall approach to learning characters, and if and how they used apps. The interviews lasted approximately 40 minutes. Interview participants included two beginner learners, four intermediate learners, and two advanced learners. Participants' levels were categorised according to their self-reports (including estimated number of characters known), experience, and any previous performance in examinations. Five of the subjects had studied or were studying Chinese as part of an undergraduate programme, two were studying Chinese for its relevance to their profession, and one was studying Chinese for personal reasons. The gender of interviewees was split equally: four males and four females.

3. Results

Nearly all (94%) of the survey respondents (N=131) indicated that they used mobile apps to support their character learning and 41% of respondents (N=57) used two or more. Figure 1 shows which apps learners reported using, with Pleco, an electronic dictionary, being the most popular app among respondents with 77% (N=108) using it. Most interviewees (7 out of 8) also used Pleco and it was clear that for those who had spent time studying in China, it had been an indispensable tool, or as one interviewee had described it: her 'friend'. Memrise and Skritter also appeared to be quite popular with 31% (N=45) and 25% (N=37) of survey respondents indicating that they employed it. Memrise offers a range of language and other courses which include ready-made flashcards with 'mems' (mnemonics) designed to help learners connect new information with what they already know. Skritter is also a flashcard tool but is specifically designed for Chinese and focuses on the writing of characters.

Figure 1. Mobile apps used for character learning

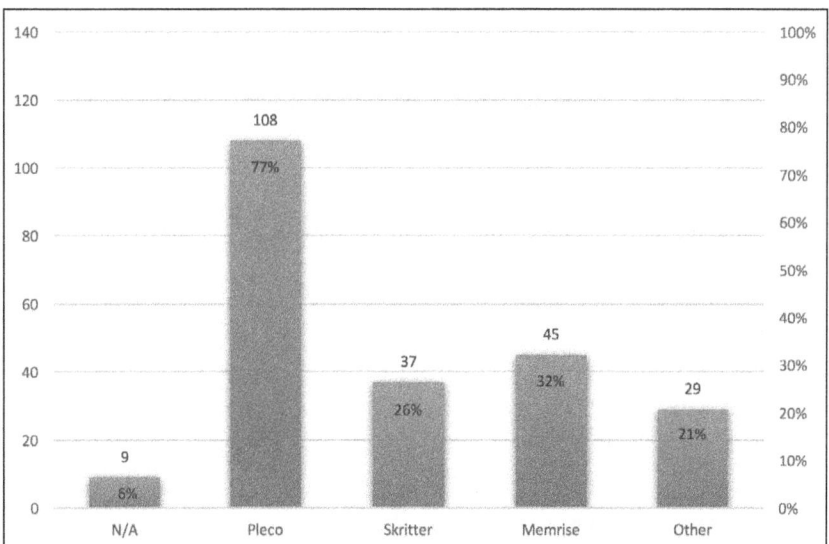

In the 'other' option, respondents listed a variety of other Chinese learning mobile apps and online resources, such as TrainChinese: Dictionary & Flash Cards, Hanping Chinese Dictionary for Android device, Youdao Translation, and Learn Chinese: Online Mandarin Course & Baidu Online Translation. When prompted, interviewees also mentioned the app Decipher, and online resources including Arch Chinese, Write Chinese, and Yellowbridge.

When asked to estimate what proportion of their character learning time was spent on apps, 58% of students (N=81) reported spending around 30 to 50% of their character learning time on mobile apps and nearly 10% (N=13) of students reported spending over 70% of their character learning time on mobile apps.

The strategies supported by apps which were employed by respondents are summarised in Table 1. The table also shows the apps students used for each strategy, with some students reporting the use of more than one app to support a particular strategy. The most commonly used mobile app-based strategies are 'viewing the stroke order of the character' and 'looking up words and sentences that contain the characters'. When the levels of learners are considered, results indicate that lower level learners most frequently used apps to identify components and listen to pronunciation while intermediate and advanced learners more frequently used apps to help them memorise new characters and to associate with previously learnt characters.

Table 1. Mobile app based Chinese character learning strategies

	Strategy	App(s) used	% Users	N=140
1	*I use an animation app to view the stroke order of the character.	Pleco, Skritter, Memrise, other	62%	88
2	*I use an app to identify the components/radicals of the character.	Pleco, Skritter, Memrise	56%	79
3	*I use an animation app to trace over the stroke order of the character.	Pleco, Skritter, Memrise	47%	66
4	I use an app to provide me with 'mems' - ways of memorising a character.	Pleco, Skritter, Memrise, other	44%	62
5	I use a dictionary app to look up words and sentences that contain the characters.	Pleco, Memrise	62%	88
6	I use an app to listen to the pronunciation of the words or characters.	Pleco, Skritter	55%	78
7	*I use an app to make flashcards with the character on one side and pinyin and the meaning on the other.	Pleco, Memrise, other	44%	63
8	*I use an app to keep a record of new characters and words.	Pleco, Memrise	50%	70
9	*I use an app to place the new word in a group with other words that are similar in some way.	Pleco, Memrise, other	39%	56
10	I check characters in an on-line dictionary or app for other meanings.	Pleco, Skritter, Memrise, other	58%	83

* indicates strategies adapted from Shen (2005)

Figure 2 shows the app-supported strategies when respondents were categorised according to level. The most popular strategies among lower level learners are to identify components (65%, N=32) and listen to pronunciation (61%,

N=30). Identifying components was also the most popular among intermediate learners (74%, N=44), while for advanced learners, the most popular app-based strategy was looking up words and sentences that contain the character (50%, N=16).

Figure 2. The use of app-based strategies according to proficiency level

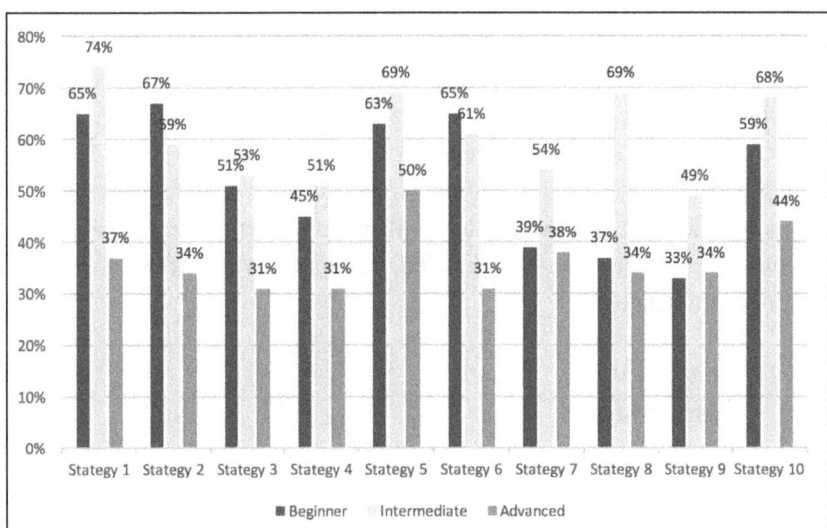

The reliability of the survey findings in relation to the apps used for a specific strategy must be considered with caution, since some of the apps do not always have the functionality learners ostensibly associated with them. The interview data did, however, support the general finding in relation to the most commonly used app-supported strategies.

A further limitation of the survey was that there was no 'other' option for students to reveal potential additional strategies. The interview data demonstrated that some of the strategies borrowed and then adapted from Shen (2005) do not reflect the potential complexity of strategy use when applied to apps. For example, the phrase 'viewing the stroke order' can involve a cluster of strategies when using an app. Learners can initially view the stroke order animation to determine or check the correct order. Subsequent viewings of the animation could also be used as a form of mechanical rehearsal either by simply watching the animation while trying to memorise the correct sequence or by following the animation and copying it using a finger in the air. One learner reported that counting the strokes during the playing of the animation might help him to recall how to write the character later.

In terms of functionality, the survey findings demonstrated that nearly 40% of respondents were using a lot of functions that apps provide. However, 45% of respondents only used one or two functions of the apps, such as using as an e-dictionary to look up meaning and sentence examples. The interview data provided further insights into this issue. Many of the interview subjects, despite the fact that they were users of Pleco, were not aware of many of its functions such as the etymology function, flashcards, stroke order animation or the Clipboard Reader.

4. Discussion

This section discusses the findings in relation to the two research questions.

- What mobile apps are used by CFL learners to learn Chinese characters?

In answering the first research question, the findings show that most students in this study are using at least one mobile app to support their character learning and that most report using them for a significant amount of their character study time. This adds further evidence to the claim that students believe learning with mobile devices can help in the learning of Chinese characters (Rosell-Aguilar & Kan, 2015). A range of different apps as well as online tools were used by students, but the electronic dictionary Pleco was the most popular. Although for many students this was their single app of choice, a large proportion of students were using a range of different digital resources. This is interesting when other studies have shown that some language learners rely on one app as their sole resource for their study (Rosell-Aguilar, 2016).

- How do CFL learners use mobile apps to learn Chinese characters?

Although there is variation among learners in how they use apps, many learners are only using them to support a few strategies and therefore employing only a small proportion of the apps' functionality. There are two main possible and interrelated reasons here. Firstly, it is likely that learners rely on a limited number of mechanical strategies in general as demonstrated by Wang (1998) and Shen (2005). Secondly, they may not be aware of how easy it is to use other strategies with an app. For example, although the survey suggested that more than half of respondents used an app to identify the components of a character, none of the interviewees who were regular users of Pleco used it to do this. In fact, they tended to avoid this strategy in general, despite the fact that all of them stated that recognising radicals or components made it easier for them to learn a new character. The general consensus among interviewees was that they had avoided focusing too much on radicals because of the cognitive overload. The extent to which radicals should be a focus of CFL teaching and learning is controversial because of this issue, but as Shen (2005) argues, and the students in this study seem to believe, knowledge of radicals is likely to facilitate character learning. An electronic dictionary such as Pleco, which enables learners to identify all the components of a character with minimal extra mental effort (just one tap), may prove a valuable tool in this respect.

The interviewees in this study were just not aware of many of the functions of the apps they were using, probably because they are not immediately obvious to the user. Students therefore may require awareness-raising as well as training. Grenfell and Harris (2015) highlighted the need for strategy instruction for CFL learners and it is argued here that such instruction should include the use of apps. This requires that teachers are familiar with a range of apps so that they can provide the appropriate support. As Kukulska-Hulme (2009) suggests, "teachers and learners must try to work together to understand how portable, wireless technologies may best be used for learning" (p. 161).

Another reason for the limited use of some of the functions of Pleco is that they are paid add-ons and students admitted that they expected apps to be free. The authors would argue that in the case of some paid-for apps, the potential for efficient learning is so great that teachers should help learners make informed purchasing decisions by demonstrating their functionality.

The findings suggest that there may be differential use of app-based strategies according to proficiency level, but conclusions cannot be drawn from the sample studied here. This could be an interesting and fruitful area for future research.

5. Conclusion

The results of this study indicate that mobile apps can play a significant role in supporting many students in their learning of Chinese characters. Pleco emerged as the most popular app for the CFL learners in this study, but most users exploited only a small proportion of its functionality, suggesting that learner training is required. Further research is needed to investigate a wider population of CFL learners and their use of apps, but also to explore the potential impact of learner training in the wider context of strategy-based instruction.

6. Acknowledgements

We owe special thanks to Ms. Peng Yuan, Mandarin tutor at International School of Xi'an Jiaotong University for distributing and collecting the questionnaires. Our gratitude also goes to the learners who took part in the interview surveys.

References

British Council. (2013). *Languages for the future*. https://www.britishcouncil.org/organisation/policy-insight-research/research/languages-future

Burston, J. (2015). Twenty years of mall project implementation: a meta-analysis of learning outcomes. *ReCALL, 27*(1), 4-20. https://doi.org/10.1017/S0958344014000159

Godwin-Jones, R. (2011). Emerging technology: mobile apps for language learning. *Language Learning and Technology, 15*(2), 2-11. http://llt.msu.edu/issues/june2011/emerging.pdf

Grenfell, M., & Harris, V. (2015). Memorisation strategies and the adolescent leaning of Mandarin Chinese as a foreign language. *Linguistics and education, 31*, 1-13.

Hanban. (2013). *Confucius Institute development plan 2012 -2013.* http://www.hanban.edu.cn/article/2013-02/28/content_486129.htm

Hanban. (2014). *Chinese tests: HSK.* http://english.hanban.org/node_8002.htm

Hu, B. (2010). The challenges of Chinese: a preliminary study of UK learners' perceptions of difficulty. *Language Learning Journal, 38*(1), 99-118. https://doi.org/10.1080/09571731003620721

Kukulska-Hulme, A. (2009). Will mobile learning change language learning? *ReCALL, 21*(2), 157-165. https://doi.org/10.1017/S0958344009000202

Levy, M., & Steel, C. (2015). Language learner perspective on the functionality and use of electronic language dictionaries. *ReCALL, 27*(2), 177-196. https://doi.org/10.1017/S095834401400038X

Nyikos, M., & Macaro, E. (2007). A review of vocabulary learning strategies: focus on language proficiency and learner voice. In A. D. Cohen & E. Macaro (Eds), *Language Learner Strategies: Thirty Years of Research and Practice* (pp 251-273). Oxford: Oxford University Press.

Oxford, R. L. (1990). *Language learning strategies: what every teacher should know*. Boston: Heinle and Heinle.

Rosell-Aguilar, F. (2016). An evaluation of a language learning app by its users. *Paper presented at the International Conference on MOOCs, Informal Language Learning and Mobility, Milton Keynes, UK, October 2016.*

Rosell-Aguilar, F., & Kan, Q. (2015). Design and user evaluation of a mobile app to teach Chinese characters. *JALT CALL Journal, 11*(1), 19-40.

Schmitt, N. (1997). Vocabulary learning strategies. In N. Schmitt & M. McCarthy (Eds), *Vocabulary: description, acquisition and pedagogy* (pp. 199-227). Cambridge University Press.

Shen, H. (2005). An investigation of Chinese-character learning strategies among non-native speakers of Chinese. *System, 33*(1), 49-68. https://doi.org/10.1016/j.system.2004.11.001

Sung, K. (2012). A study on Chinese-character learning strategies and character learning performance among American learners of Chinese. *Chinese as a Second Language Research, 1*(2), 193-210. https://doi.org/10.1515/caslar-2012-0012

Sung, K., & Wu. H. (2011). Factors influencing the learning of Chinese characters. *International Journal of Bilingual Education and Bilingualism, 14*(6), 683-700. https://doi.org/10.1080/14790718.2010.532555

Wang, S. (1998). A study on the learning and teaching of Hanzi-Chinese characters. *Working Papers in Educational Linguistics, 14*(1), 69-101.

10. English at your fingertips: learning initiatives for rural areas

Lilit Bekaryan[1], Zaruhi Soghomonyan[2], and Arusyak Harutyunyan[3]

Abstract

The present paper addresses the practice of a new English classroom on the model of a free e-learning programme in the context of adult education in Armenia, a country where English is taught as a second foreign language. The research reviews the results and impact of an online English language learning programme initiated for those vulnerable groups who have restricted access to English language resources. The research is built on qualitative data collected through the analysis of evaluation questionnaires and reflection exercises administered on the completion of the course. The aspects explored include the reasons for the high level of dropouts, the importance of maintaining social presence in the virtual learning environment, the learners' cognitive frustration caused by the use of the inductive approach (namely guided discovery on an online platform), and the activities that can foster communication among the learners and encourage them to build a strong and supportive community. Taken together, the results highlight the importance of administering pre-course surveys, adjusting the teaching methodology to the learners' past learning experience and maintaining interaction among the learners. The research will benefit teaching English as a foreign language specialists and curriculum designers engaged in the

1. Yerevan State University, Yerevan, Armenia; lilitelt@gmail.com

2. French University in Armenia, Yerevan, Armenia; zarasoghomonyan@gmail.com

3. International Scientific-Educational Center of NAS RA, Yerevan, Armenia; arusyakharutyunyan@yahoo.com

How to cite this chapter: Bekaryan, L., Soghomonyan, Z., & Harutyunyan, A. (2017). English at your fingertips: learning initiatives for rural areas. In Q. Kan & S. Bax (Eds), *Beyond the language classroom: researching MOOCs and other innovations* (pp. 113-125). Research-publishing.net. https://doi.org/10.14705/rpnet.2017.mooc2016.675

field of online teaching. The results of the research will be invested in improving the overall quality of the further stages of the programme.

Keywords: online education, online course, online English teaching and learning, student motivation, student dropout.

1. Introduction

Recent learning technologies have led to new opportunities in the field of English language instruction in regions with limited teaching resources. Though being in the spotlight of modern education, online teaching still poses challenges for educators, ranging from a high rate of dropouts (Onah, Sinclair, & Boyatt, 2014), the argument of whether online learners perform as well as those engaged in face-to-face education (Dutton, Dutton, & Perry, 1999), or to the relevance of designing lesson plans for the virtual environment.

In the present paper, an attempt is made to address the generic and specific problems experienced by the team of presenters in the capacity of online course designers and teachers in the context of rural Armenia.

2. Context

In 2014, the US Embassy in Yerevan came up with the *Expanding English Access: Reaching Remote Regions with New Technologies* programme that envisaged teaching English in Armenia's remote regions by offering a blended course of two online and one face-to-face weekly sessions to post-high school youth in hard-to-reach towns. The main goal of the programme was to create a resilient and growing economic environment through improving English knowledge among adults in regions of Armenia. The programme sought to increase competitiveness and address unemployment by building the language skills required to create small and medium enterprises and to expand opportunities for trade and investment. The programme targeted 17-35 year olds, a demographic group that had no access to classroom resources or instruction if not attending university classes.

The first online course was delivered synchronously with live sessions usually following the same format. The sessions started with a short introductory talk to highlight the target language and the specific language issues that learners needed to consider. The learners were then set a task which they performed after viewing the video about the target communication situation. Afterwards, they responded to the statements on the screen providing answers to the questions or voicing their opinions. Whenever time and the internet connection permitted, this response elicitation took place live online with a learner or a group of learners sharing their video with the whole community online. There was also elicitation of comments in the chat thread. The sessions were usually concluded with the assignment of the offline task to be completed before the next online session. The live sessions took place twice a week, and once a week the learners joined face-to-face instruction in their local groups.

The first round of online classes was launched in 2014, reaching about 100 users. Unfortunately, technical problems, such as low internet penetration or system lapses, were frequent during the first four sessions. Classes were hosted online synchronously in OpenMeetings, a software used for video conferencing, instant messaging, whiteboard, and collaborative document editing. The intended English level of the targeted audience ranged from complete beginners to B1.

Overall, around 120 participants from four different regions participated in this programme, and 88 out of 120 graduated with an improved knowledge of English. Several participants benefited by finding a new job, or using more resources in English during their studies.

Having been considered a success, the programme was followed by a second one in 2016, targeting ten regions with 200 registered participants. The new programme involved one live session per week hosted in OpenMeetings for all the participants and introduced them to the target language of the session, a

Chapter 10

two-hour session in Moodle, an open source learning platform that could be accessed at any time (convenient for the users), and an interactive webinar in OpenMeetings for a group of students from the same area. The whole course was divided into four modules, each lasting six weeks. All weekly live sessions were hosted by the course content creators and main teachers. The teachers who shared the same location with the learners managed the interactive webinars over the weekend, consolidating the content they had covered throughout the week. It is worth mentioning that in the second round of the programme, face-to-face meetings were administered every six weeks, being further apart as compared to the first round of the programme. This was because the programme mainly focused on raising the awareness of learning technologies among the residents in rural areas, so a decision was made to reduce the number of face-to-face meetings.

Every six weeks, the participants met in their local group for a two hour face-to-face meeting with their local teacher to discuss any open questions and revise the language of the past sessions. The first round was followed by an immediate reflection exercise initiated to assemble data at factual, contextual and affective levels to improve the experience of the second phase.

3. Method

The evaluation of the project was approached from qualitative and quantitative perspectives. The main evaluation tools included an end-of-course survey completed by 60 participants and informal interviews on the phone with 40 participants who had withdrawn from the project. During the interviews, the learners cited the main reasons for their withdrawal and during the survey they reported what they had found useful about the course, their learning experience overall, and which aspects they would like to see improved if a similar project was hosted. The data collected from the survey aimed to help the teams of teachers and syllabus designers to recognise the problems the participants experienced throughout the project and tackle them in their practice. At the same time, throughout the project, methods of statistical data analysis were used to keep track of the participants' performance, participation, and progress, both in the Moodle and synchronous sessions.

4. Research findings

Despite its versatile format and content, the second phase was more challenging in terms of participant engagement and performance than the first one. To determine the quality and effectiveness of the programme, several factors were examined through the surveys and interviews, among them the participants' dropout rates, completion rate of Moodle lessons, and learners' presence and performance in online sessions and in face-to-face meetings.

4.1. Participation types

Our analysis of the data suggested that our participants demonstrated three types of engagement in the course: moodle-based, face-to-face, and live.

Figure 1. Participation types in percentages

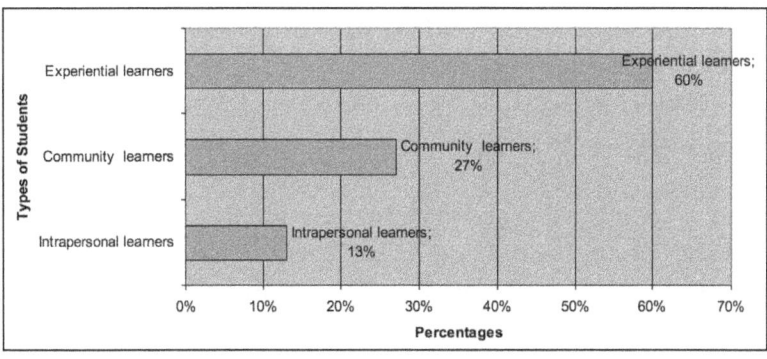

Interestingly, the presence of the participants and their engagement in the course varied depending on their preferred mode of instruction. Hence, the survey suggested that a classification be made between (a) intrapersonal learners, who, being introspective and independent, preferred moodle-based instruction,

(b) experiential learners, who gave preference to face-to-face sessions, as they appreciated constant feedback on their work, and (c) *community* learners who shared the same beliefs about learning, demonstrating a high level of participation in live sessions. Overall, as the statistical data demonstrate, the number of community learners exceeded that of the intrapersonal learners by 14% (Figure 1). Moreover, the number of experiential participants proved to be the highest.

4.2. Retention and dropouts

Most online educators recognise the challenge of learner retention. Research suggests that approximately 70% of adult learners enrolled in an online programme do not complete it and that the dropout rate of learners engaged in online courses is higher than that of students attending face-to face courses (Meister, 2002). Though some researchers might associate a high dropout rate with a failure in online education, others (e.g. Diaz, 2002) argue that the factors affecting the dropout decision are not subject to any control and a high dropout rate is not necessarily indicative of academic non-success.

In our case, 115 out of 200 registered participants joined the first module, of which five participants withdrew from the second module. There were only 110 participants both in the second and third modules and 30 learners dropped out in the final module of the course. Hence, throughout the whole project, 120 people had dropped out of the original 200.

Figure 2 below shows the completion rate per modules in the given course. As we can see, figures look more positive for Modules 1 and 2. At the same time, fewer participants joined Module 3, and their participation ratio in Module 4 almost reached a quarter. In this respect, it seems appropriate to look into the possible reasons for the participants' dropouts.

Gibson (1998) identifies student-related factors, educational factors and situational factors accounting for the students withdrawing their participation from distance courses. While student-related factors include the learners' educational preparation, motivation, and student learning style, educational ones deal with the quality and complexity of educational materials and the provision of tutorial support. Finally, situational factors are related to the changes in life circumstances, family and work. In this programme, for instance, 18% of the learners quit simply because the pressure at work was too high.

Figure 2. Course completion rate per module

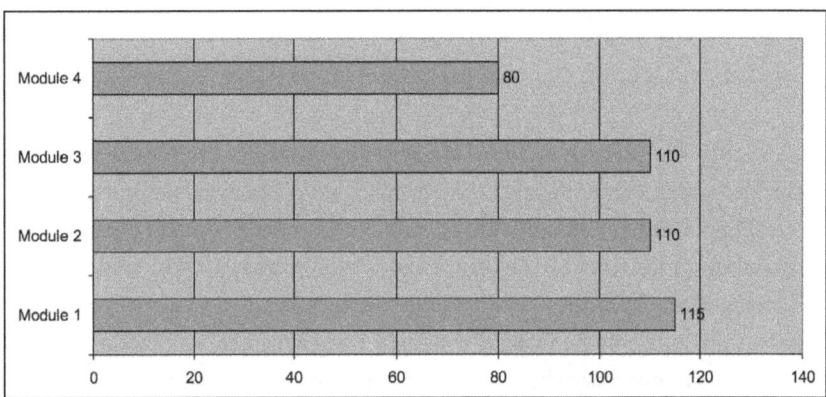

Other reasons for the high rate of dropouts in online courses cited by researchers (e.g. Onah et al., 2014) include lack of time, insufficient instructor support, computer illiteracy and course complexity. All of these factors impede the learners' motivation and discourage their participation in online courses.

Figure 3 below illustrates the key reasons for dropouts in the present programme, based on the results of the survey administered among all the participants of the course upon the completion of Round 2.

The percentage of the learners who never accessed the course made up 17%, while most learners (47%) appeared to have quit the course for technical reasons. 18% of dropouts are ascribed to student-related or situational factors, such as a sudden loss of motivation or migration to another country due to the high level of unemployment among the working age population. As we can see from the chart, situational factors outweigh the educational ones.

Figure 3. Reasons for dropouts

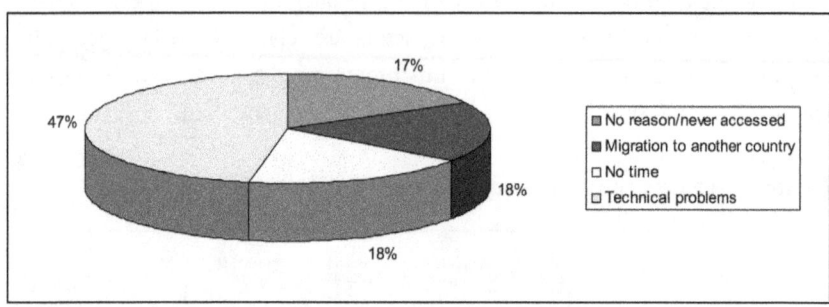

Interestingly, the geographic locations of the teachers also seem to be related to the dropout rates. Out of the nine local teachers involved in the programme, only two teachers were not directly located in the area their group participants came from and the groups managed by these teachers collected the most dropouts. The teachers teaching in those sites where their learners were located maintained not only *instructional* communication with their learners, entailing synchronous and asynchronous online activities such as discussion forums, live sessions, home assignments or group discussions related to the mechanics and content of the course, but also social communication. As the culture of online communication does not enjoy much popularity with the residents of rural areas in Armenia, teachers were able to communicate with their learners either by phone or during the occasional encounters in the area. The physical proximity also enabled the teachers to be in regular contact with their learners, reminding them to attend their online classes and not to miss the live sessions hosted by the main teacher. The instructor-led communication transformed into a social one where the learners could initiate both virtual and face-to-face interaction with their local teachers. This encouraged the learners to feel both emotionally and personally connected to the group they adhered to. Informal chats with the learners and their comments in forums showed that the course shared this sense of belonging within their local regional group and their participation in the course was more successful and effective. In the two remaining groups whose teachers came from other towns and cities, this social communication was weaker, and hence the learners' motivation to continue the course was affected.

A post-course satisfaction survey was carried out among the participants who successfully completed the course in Module 4. Figure 4 below shows the regional representation of participants per groups from eight regions in Armenia.

Figure 4. Regional representation

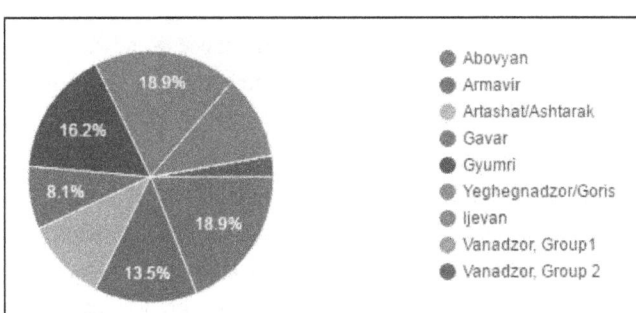

During the survey, over 94% of the respondents stated they would recommend this course to their family members, friends and colleagues, while around 60% of the respondents stated that the course had met their expectations and they would definitely recommend it to their community. Some respondents also came up with their suggestions on the next stage of the project: "Thank you for such an interesting and useful English course. The course was really interactive. Looking forward to the next one" (Gohar, 21).

4.3. Programme evaluation

Among the most important drawbacks the team highlighted was the lack of a pre-course survey with the aim of understanding what participants' expectations and needs were. It has been repeatedly ascertained that the use of pre-course surveys allows the instructors to assess students' prior knowledge and expectations. In this particular case, there was no pre-course survey due to the low budget and insufficient resources of the project. We are inclined to think that in case student expectations had been revealed, it would have been possible not only to adapt the course design to the needs of the course participants, but also to retain more students.

Another lesson learnt was the inefficient organization of socialising activities, which resulted in loose attachment of the learners to the course. Throughout recent years, with the emergence of a myriad of online courses offered by top-ranking universities, more and more research is being conducted with the aim of revealing the components that are necessary to ensure a high level of retention among the participants of e-learning courses. Findings suggest that building a community in an online course impacts student success and retention. Students feel more comfortable and less isolated when developing a sense of belonging to a certain community (Paul, 2013).

Upon the start of the second phase, an attempt was made at building rapport and a sense of community among the learners by asking them to post something about themselves and to comment on the posts of at least two other learners. However, since the number of participants was high and no grade was given to forum participation, some of the learners would not post or comment, thus encouraging isolation. The teaching team addressed this issue by being constantly present and commenting on the posts, since based on their classroom experience they knew that most Armenian learners, who are used to traditional schooling and are prone to viewing online courses as something superficial, welcome instructor comments and/or intervention, as it makes them feel heard and evaluated. This approach worked and enhanced the learners' participation in forums.

As far as teaching methods and methodologies are concerned, it is worth mentioning that the Guided-Discovery[4] (GD), a technique which is believed to be a successful inductive approach and is advocated by English language teaching experts and professionals, did not work well with this particular group of learners. Trying to reduce their teacher talking time in live sessions, teachers occasionally resorted to the use of GD when eliciting the target language for the participants not to act as passive listeners and join the discussions. Though the learners were quite active and seemed to be quite enthusiastic about the procedure as a whole, post-course surveys came to prove the reverse. When assessing the instructors' performance, the learners (80%) reported their

---

4. A technique where a teacher provides examples of a language item and helps the learners to find the rules themselves; see https://www.teachingenglish.org.uk/article/guided-discovery

discomfort and frustration over the teacher(s) not teaching them anything but demanding that they work out the rules and answers on their own. This leads us again to the issue of addressing the learners' learning experience to be able to plan and deliver a lesson that would meet their expectations and learning styles. As we know, a GD problem must be adequately scaffolded to be successful in the classroom (Hmelo-Silver, Duncan, & Chinn, 2007) for the learners to remain within their zone of proximal development, the zone between what they can do on their own and what they cannot do, even with help (Vygotsky, 1978). In our case, the scaffolding stage was not completely successful, as though a placement language test had been administered upon the start of the course, the learners' past learning experience and expectations had not been considered. The next stage of the project, however, will consider a needs analysis not only as a pre-stage for the course design, but as an ongoing process targeted at improving the delivery of the course.

5. Conclusion

The results of this study provide some important insights into the cognitive and psychological effects of virtual instruction. Contrary to what we expected, the methods that seem to work quite well in face-to-face instruction might not prove to be as effective in the virtual environment. In this respect, it will help to consider the learning background and the past experience of the course participants before planning and delivering the course.

To build a resilient learner community, it is recommended that the format of the learning experience be more group-based rather than self-paced through the implementation of pair and/or group programmes to develop the sense of community belonging among the learners and hence foster their motivation. It is also suggested that future courses feature an online map of Armenia with the participants' home locations highlighted to illustrate how many people from every region in Armenia are attending the course. If the software permits, the map will help keep track of the improvement the participants are making and show which community enjoys the highest rates in terms of activity, module completion and overall progress. This will encourage the learners to work more effectively towards a common goal they share.

Despite dropouts being an unavoidable element of any online course, it might be appropriate to tackle this problem in advance to the course delivery and to request that the enrolled participants sign an agreement stating their commitment to the course. An extended orientation stage for learners to familiarise themselves with the format of the virtual learning environment might also help the learners avoid technical problems. Finally, introducing a clear grading system will encourage the learners to contribute to the forums and online discussions.

When the aforementioned challenges are overcome, it is anticipated that the *Reaching Remote Regions with New Technologies* programme will enrich their growth potential, capacity building, and exert a stronger impact on vulnerable communities in Armenia.

6. Acknowledgements

This research would not have been possible without the support of the US Embassy in Yerevan and Children of Armenia Foundation (COAF) in Armenia. We would like to extend our gratitude to Hasmik Mikayelyan from the US Embassy to Armenia and our colleagues from COAF, Tatevik Nalbandyan and Suzanne Khachatryan for sharing their feedback with us and for hosting a post-course survey[5] among the participants. Their feedback assisted our research, although they may not agree with all of the conclusions in the present paper.

References

Diaz, D. P. (2002). Online drop rates revisited. *The Technology Source Archives*. http://technologysource.org/article/online_drop_rates_revisited/

---

5. Available from https://research-publishing.box.com/s/tj2815v34azssk7bz1gtqalrdy03cp8t

Dutton, J., Dutton, M., & Perry, J. (1999). *Do online students perform as well as lecture students?* North Carolina State University. https://onlinelearningconsortium.org/jaln_full_issue/volume-6-issue-1-july-2002/

Gibson, C. C. (1998). The distance learner's academic self-concept. In C. Gibson (Ed.), *Distance learners in higher education: institutional responses for quality outcomes* (pp. 65-76). Madison, WI: Atwood.

Hmelo-Silver, C. E., Duncan, R. G., & Chinn, C. A. (2007). Scaffolding and achievement in problem-based and inquiry learning: a response to Kirschner, Sweller, and Clark (2006). *Educational Psychologist, 4*(2), 99-107. https://doi.org/10.1080/00461520701263368

Meister, J. (2002). *Pillars of e-learning success*. New York: Corporate University Exchange.

Onah, D. F. O., Sinclair, J., Boyatt, R. (2014). Dropout rates of massive open online courses: behavioural patterns. In *Proceedings of the 6th International Conference on Education and New Learning Technologies (EDULEARN14), Barcelona, Spain*. https://www2.warwick.ac.uk/fac/sci/dcs/people/research/csrmaj/daniel_onah_edulearn14.pdf

Paul, A. M. (2013, January, 21). *Do you feel like you belong? Why it matters for learning.* http://time.com/4108632/yale-controversy-belonging/

Vygotsky, L. S. (1978). *Mind in society: the development of higher psychological processes.* Cambridge, MA: Harvard University Press.

11. The language exchange programme: plugging the gap in formal learning

Tita Beaven[1], Mara Fuertes Gutiérrez[2], and Anna Motzo[3]

Abstract

In the context of distance language learning, speaking is frequently perceived as the most challenging skill; this paper reports on a 12 week summer language exchange programme providing students with new ways of practising their oral abilities. Students who completed an undergraduate beginners' language module took part in regular online, synchronous language exchange sessions with a partner. This paper analyses the impact of taking part in a language exchange task on the students' motivation. The mixed methods research included an activity perception questionnaire (based on Deci, Eghrari, Patrick, & Leone, 1994) to investigate the motivation of participants whilst undertaking a specific language exchange session, as well as qualitative data from both the questionnaire and the project discussion forum. The language exchange programme provides the opportunity for learners to take ownership of their learning and personalise it, and functions as a bridge between formal and informal learning. However, despite the enjoyment and interest provided by this type of experience, it is not without stress, and requires self-determination and autonomy to result in a positive and sustainable learning experience.

Keywords: online language learning, intrinsic motivation, language exchange, formal and informal learning.

---

1. The Open University, Milton Keynes, United Kingdom; tita.beaven@open.ac.uk

2. The Open University, Milton Keynes, United Kingdom; mara.fuertes-gutierrez@open.ac.uk

3. The Open University, Milton Keynes, United Kingdom; a.motzo@open.ac.uk

How to cite this chapter: Beaven, T., Fuertes Gutiérrez, M., & Motzo, A. (2017). The language exchange programme: plugging the gap in formal learning. In Q. Kan & S. Bax (Eds), *Beyond the language classroom: researching MOOCs and other innovations* (pp. 127-140). Research-publishing.net. https://doi.org/10.14705/rpnet.2017.mooc2016.676

Chapter 11

1. Introduction

Motivation and self-determination are crucial to successful language learning (Dörnyei, 2003; Dörnyei & Ushioda, 2013). The affordances of the new technologies and social media allow language learners to expand their learning beyond geographical boundaries and beyond formal learning settings. In language learning, examples of this expansion of the learning environment can be evidenced in the growing popularity in the use of new language-learning tools, such as apps or games, among others. Because of this new practice, there are enhanced possibilities for learners to personalise their learning experience by choosing relevant content and by embedding informal practices into formal learning (Hall, 2009; McLoughlin & Lee, 2010). This has implications for educators, whose role in this context becomes that of facilitating a personalised learning experience that fosters independent learning skills and self-regulation as well as supporting students in identifying effective resources to practise their language skills autonomously.

A language exchange (or language tandem) is a way for language learners to practise their skills informally: two people learning each other's language meet, either face-to-face or online, and interact for an agreed period of time in one language and then in the other, usually with no pre-established syllabus or activities (Ahn, 2016). Language exchanges have been a feature of language education for over 40 years and originally took place either face-to-face or by email (for an overview of earlier studies, see Voller & Pickard, 1996). However, with the advent of online synchronous communication technology, these exchanges now often take place online, using VoIP (Voice over Internet Protocol) technologies such as Skype. Partners practise conversation, vocabulary, pronunciation and intonation, and develop their intercultural skills. Reciprocity is an important aspect of language exchanges, both in the setup of the session, and because language exchanges depend, to some extent, on learners creating opportunities for their own and their partner's learning that meet each other's needs (Ahn, 2016).

Tandems and e-tandems have been extensively analysed (Cziko, 2004; Lewis & Walker, 2003; Vassallo & Telles, 2006); other researchers (Brammerts, 2003;

Guth & Helm, 2010; O'Dowd, 2007) also discuss language exchanges as sites of intercultural learning. Research has also centred on learner-to-learner interaction and feedback (Bruen & Sudhershan, 2015), motivation and engagement (Bruen & Sudhershan, 2015) and the impact of participating in a tandem to improve language, intercultural and digital skills (Gajek, 2014; see also Pomino & Gil-Salom, 2016). As Dooly and O'Dowd (2012) highlight, a possible reason for the interest in language exchanges in so much recent research and practice stems from the fact that this approach enables the creation of spaces for intercultural exchange which combine the development of both foreign language competence and e-literacies. Moreover, such spaces also enable the practice of "multiply-integrated language competences, wherein learning is understood as an organic process, fostered through cognitively challenging, meaningful use of language" (Dooly & O'Dowd, 2012, p. 14).

This paper investigates the intrinsic motivation and self-determination of learners participating in a language exchange and the relationship between motivation, perceived competence, stress, and enjoyment in this context. Participants had completed a beginner's language course (up to A2 CEFR[4]) with The Open University (a distance learning university in the UK) and volunteered for the language exchange programme. In order to measure intrinsic motivation and self-determination, the study used research instruments based on a family of surveys created around the Intrinsic Motivation Inventory (IMI) (Deci & Ryan, 1985; Ryan, 1982). Within self-determination theory, the IMI is a well-tested evaluation instrument used to assess participants' intrinsic motivation and self-determination. According to Salkind (2008),

> "to be self-determined is to endorse one's actions with a full sense of choice and volition. When self-determined, individuals experience a sense of freedom to do what is interesting, personally important, and vitalizing, they experience themselves as self-regulating agents of their own behavior. Thus, self-determination signifies the experience of choice and endorsement of the actions in which one is engaged" (p. 2).

---

4. Common European Framework of Reference for languages (Council of Europe, 2001).

2. Methodology

2.1. Context

The programme ran for 12 weeks, and students were requested to find a language partner in order to practise their language independently. The recommended platform was *italki*, a language teachers' marketplace, which also enables users to find language partners for free (https://www.italki.com/partners), although students could also find partners elsewhere if they preferred. During the first week, the project team introduced the concept of language exchange and provided advice on where to find partners. They also provided some resources specially developed by the team to help learners prepare for and run the language exchanges. These were based around a collection of questions organised by topic appropriate for learners at level A2 of the CEFR. Participants had access to short weekly videos, some instructional (discussing effective strategies to conduct language exchanges) and some motivational (sharing tips on how to keep interested and overcome potential difficulties). An online discussion forum enabled students to share their experiences of the programme. No other form of formal language learning instruction was provided.

2.2. Participants

Participants were recruited on a voluntary basis amongst students who had just completed a beginners' course in Italian or Spanish at The Open University. A total of 31 students volunteered and were invited to complete a survey by email. There was a 29% response rate (nine students), with one incomplete survey, giving a total of eight respondents. Four of the respondents were studying Spanish and five were studying Italian. These participants only interacted with each other in the online forum. None of the language partners of these students were surveyed.

Respondents to the survey were equally distributed with regards to levels of education and employment. The most significant differences were in gender (six males and two females), age (two were between 46 and 55 years old, whereas six were 56 and over), and ethnicity (seven white, one mixed). A possible meaningful parameter is the male-female ratio, as women represented 58% of the initial participants in the study, with only 16.6% of them completing the survey, whereas 46% of the men who started the language exchange responded. However, this does not necessarily mean that the attrition rate for women was higher than for men, as that was not specifically monitored in this study. In future studies, it may be worth trying to specifically track and analyse these differences (e.g. attrition rate by gender) in order to assess whether they have any significance in terms of motivation in participating in a language exchange.

2.3. Research instruments

The mixed methods study combined quantitative and qualitative approaches to generate data. To investigate the motivation of participants whilst undertaking a specific language exchange session, we used an activity perception questionnaire (based on Deci et al., 1994), adapted to the specific context of the study.

Like the IMI, the activity perception questionnaire includes a number of statements, linked to four thematic subscales. Participants rated their response using a five point Likert scale according to their experience whilst carrying out a particular task. The authors used only three of the four subscales in the original questionnaire: (1) interest/enjoyment, a self-report measure of intrinsic motivation (Wigfield & Eccles, 2000), (2) perceived competence, a positive predictor of both self-reported and behavioural measures of intrinsic motivation, and (3) pressure/tension, a negative predictor of intrinsic motivation. The fourth subscale, perceived choice, was not used in this study. Participants filled in the 18 item questionnaire immediately after finishing a session with their language partner in order to gauge their perception of the exchange and record their immediate feedback on the experience. Participants were also administered another, longer questionnaire based on the IMI at the end of the intervention to evaluate their intrinsic motivation; in this paper, we have focused on the open comments of that final survey. Both tools also had open-ended questions to allow respondents to expand on their answers and reflect on their practice.

Chapter 11

3. Results and findings

3.1. Results of the activity perception questionnaire

Figure 1 shows the average values of the overall participant responses (n=8) in relation to the three subscales used. Numbers 1 to 5 on the vertical axis indicate the five possible responses on the Likert scale (1 = completely disagree, 3 (highlighted with the thicker line) = neither agree nor disagree, 5 = completely agree). Interest and enjoyment, the main self-report measure of intrinsic motivation (Deci & Ryan, 1985), scored 4.14, higher than perceived competence and pressure/tension: this suggests that overall, participants enjoyed the learning exchange session they had just undertaken despite feeling slightly anxious and perceiving themselves as less than competent.

Figure 1.   Average survey results for all eight respondents

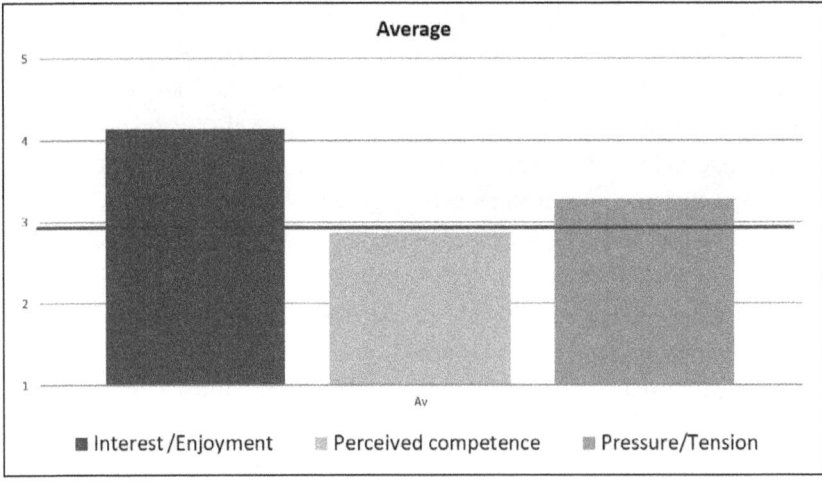

However, as shown in Figure 2, there is great variety in the perception of the experience of individual respondents. Indeed, Figure 2 shows the same data as Figure 1, but the responses here are per student, rather than on average. As in Figure 1, numbers 1 to 5 on the vertical axis indicate the five possible response on the Likert scale. It is evident that the majority of the students found the language exchange interesting and enjoyable (with Students 1 and 3 expressing the greatest interest and enjoyment). However, almost all respondents recorded greater than average levels of pressure and tension, indicating that the experience was not stress-free. Finally, it appears that there was no relation between the participants' perceived competence and their interest and enjoyment, with Student 3 feeling the exchange was highly interesting/enjoyable and also feeling competent in his/her abilities, whilst Student 1 felt the exchange was equally interesting/enjoyable in spite of not feeling very competent.

Figure 2. Survey responses per student compared to average values (Av), Students numbered 1 to 8

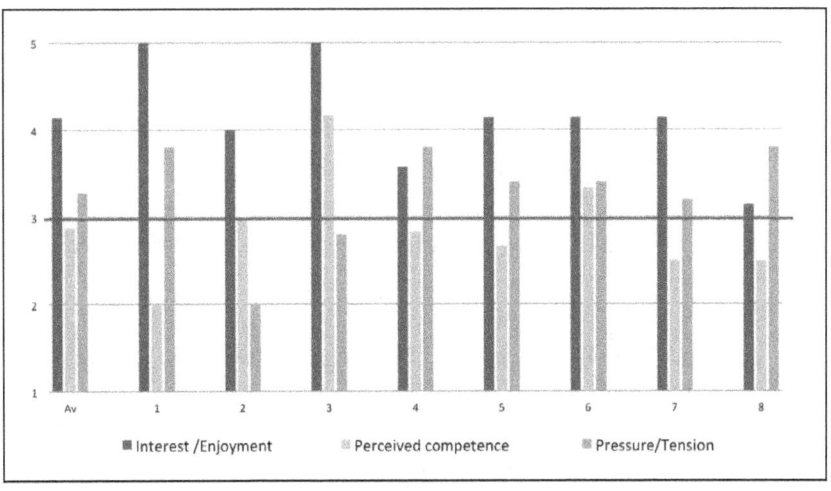

As shown in Figure 3, when it comes to perceived competence, participants felt less satisfied with their performance in terms of fluency and accuracy, and felt most competent at dealing with the technology needed to take part in the exchange. This is perhaps not surprising amongst students at a distance university who rely on technology for their studies but who have limited opportunities to practise their speaking skills with others.

Figure 3. Survey responses for the items on perceived competence

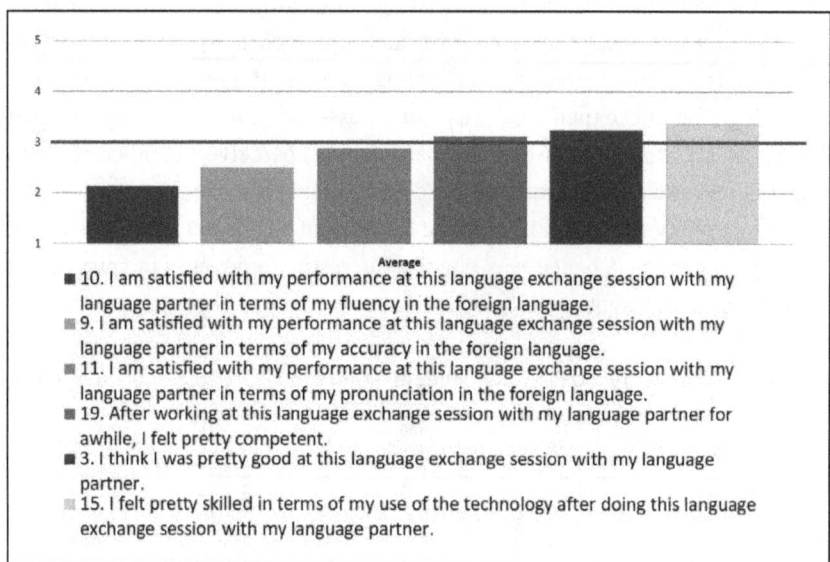

3.2. Results from open-ended questions

In addition, examples from the open-ended questions on the survey shed some light on the students' responses above.

What did you do during this language exchange session with your language partner?

> "I had prepared two topics: (a) We discussed 'ferragosto'. What my languages partner did during the day. How people generally spent this public holiday. What traditional meals they have etc. (b) We spoke about my recent visit to Battle, I tried to revise names of shops, and speak a little about the Battle of Hastings. Unbelievably, this took up nearly 30 minutes. I asked many questions in Italian. My kind language partner replied in very clear and slow Italian" (Student 3).

How did you prepare for this language exchange session with your language partner?

> "As we had to cancel the previous session because of Ferragosto, I used this public holiday as my topic for the next session. I mainly used the Italian Wikipedia (https://it.wikipedia.org/wiki/Ferragosto and https://it.wikipedia.org/wiki/Battle (East_Sussex)) to find out more about the battle as well as the public holiday, its history, customs and traditions in Italian. I also used the website as an aide mémoire/'filo conduttore' to structure my conversation. The preparation took quite a bit of time (2 hours). I think this total immersion is very beneficial for comprehension" (Student 3).

What did you do during this language exchange session with your language partner?

> "We spoke to each other in our respective languages. He is better at English than I am at Italian. We have exchanged short written texts by email and then sent each other corrections" (Student 8).

How did you prepare for this language exchange session with your language partner?

> "Very little. I am unsure as to what would be the best thing to do to prepare. A little more guidance […] on this point would help" (Student 8).

4. Discussion

In this section, we focus our discussion on the responses of two students (Student 3 and Student 8) who, as shown in Figure 4 below, appear to have evaluated their experiences quite differently.

Figure 4. Comparison between average responses, Student 3 and Student 8

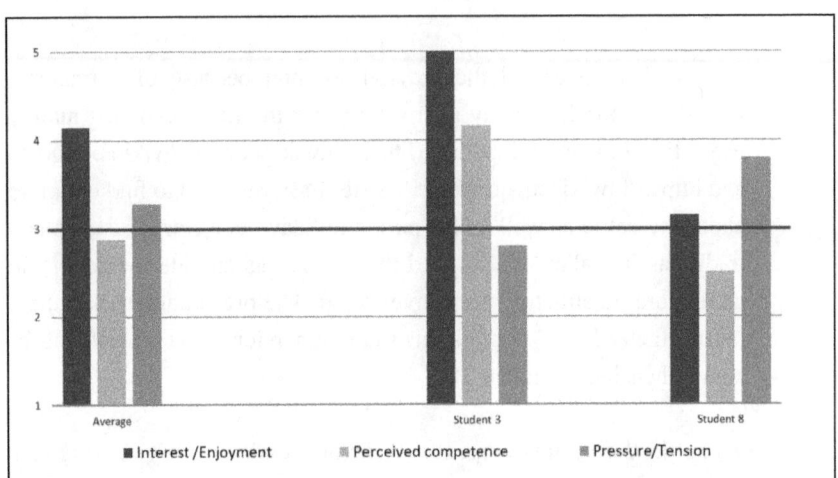

Figure 4 suggests that Student 3 had a positive learning experience; he felt fairly competent and any pressure/tension experienced did not unduly interfere with the enjoyment of the task. Conversely, Student 8 felt a high level of pressure/tension and this might have affected the level of enjoyment and his low level of perceived competence.

What is evidenced here is that Student 3 had a positive experience of this learning activity, which might be due to how much he prepared prior to the language exchange session. Student 3 showed a high level of autonomy and self-determination by selecting two relevant topics and setting time for preparation; he also personalised his learning by using topics that were of interest and relevant to him and his partner (Ferragosto is the most important summer event in Italy). Student 3 sought and found suitable resource material on Wikipedia, a process which enabled him to build up vocabulary and learn appropriate structures which he then used during the language exchange session. By doing so, we argue that his intrinsic motivation was reinforced by the experience: Student 3 demonstrated to be in control of his own learning and gave evidence of being a self-regulated and autonomous learner.

On the contrary, Student 8 did not enjoy the language exchange session as much, and we argue that his lack of preparation prior to the language exchange session might have contributed to him not feeling particularly competent and therefore tense. Student 8 seemed to be slightly overwhelmed by the perception that his language partner was better than him, rather than making the most of what such a situation can offer. Finally, although the research team produced a bank of resources to support learners, Student 8 thought there was not enough guidance, indicating that perhaps he had not engaged with the resources as much as other students, and that he did not have the autonomy to find his own resources for the session either. Furthermore, the analysis of other qualitative data at the end of the programme suggests that, although it was not an unqualified positive experience (one student said this sort of work, whilst interesting, was not really for them), three of the participants said that it had improved their confidence. Three students also remarked that they had found it a good experience despite it being slightly stressful, showing the importance of resilience in making the exchange a success:

> "It started by being nerve-wracking and surreal but ended with it being really good experience. […]" (Student 4).

> "I really enjoyed the language exchange programme but was very nervous at taking part" (Student 3).

> "Great fun, a real challenge, but I have been very fortunate in that my Italian partner is very keen to learn English, and is a little better at English than I am at Italian! It is still quite daunting at the start of each session" (Student 6).

Some participants reported on their intercultural encounters, commenting on the motivation of practising the language with a speaker of that language, which also provided a glimpse into their culture:

> "I believe I have not only met a very nice person, but I am also learning Italian. This method of improving your language skills gives you a

direct 'glimpse' into the life of your language partner, his/her culture and everyday concerns" (Student 1).

"For me it has opened a completely new window into Italy and its people. It will inspire me to continue my Italian studies with more enthusiasm and drive" (Student 2).

5. Conclusion

Language exchange programmes can be a bridge between formal and informal language learning and practice. New technologies enable learners to expand and take control of their learning outside the formal learning environment, and personalise it.

This study sheds new light on the relationship between intrinsic motivation, enjoyment, and tension in online self-directed learning; however, it also presents some limitations as the sample was small. Our findings indicate that the adult learners seemed to find enjoyment and interest, and therefore motivation, in a task that they also found somewhat stressful, which we read as evidence of their resilience. As our analysis of the two students indicates, a regular language exchange is difficult to sustain without the ability to learn autonomously. Factors such as intrinsic motivation and self-determination, i.e. the ability to continue doing something that is 'interesting, personally important, and vitalising' despite the tensions this might produce, are likely to impact on the overall learning experience.

Future research could be conducted into whether younger learners or learners in other settings (e.g. face-to-face) also feel language exchanges are motivating and/or stressful, and whether they have the resilience to succeed in this mode of learning. For practitioners, there is also a need to develop strategies and resources to support their students in becoming better self-directed learners in order to enjoy the benefits of language exchanges.

6. Acknowledgements

This research was funded by the Strategic Scholarship Fund, Faculty of Education and Language Studies, The Open University, summer 2016.

References

Ahn, T. Y. (2016). Learner agency and the use of affordances in language-exchange interactions. *Language and Intercultural Communication, 16*(2), 164-181. https://doi.org/10.1080/14708477.2015.1125911

Brammerts, H. (2003). Autonomous language learning in tandem: the development of a concept. In T. Lewis & L. Walker (Eds), *Autonomous language learning in tandem* (pp.27-36). Sheffield: Academy Electronic Publications.

Bruen, J., & Sudhershan, A. (2015). "So They're Actually Real?" Integrating e-tandem learning into the study of language for international business. *Journal of Teaching in International Business, 26*(2), 81-93. https://doi.org/10.1080/08975930.2014.993009

Council of Europe. (2001). *Common European framework of reference for languages*. Cambridge: Cambridge University Press.

Cziko, G. (2004). Electronic tandem language learning (e-tandem): a third approach to second language learning for the 21st century. *Calico Journal, 22*(1), 26-39.

Deci, E. L., Eghrari, H., Patrick, B. C., & Leone, D. (1994). Facilitating internalization: the self-determination theory perspective. *Journal of Personality, 62*, 119-142. https://doi.org/10.1111/j.1467-6494.1994.tb00797.x

Deci, E. L., & Ryan, R. M. (1985). *Intrinsic motivation and self-determination in human behavior*. New York: Plenum. https://doi.org/10.1007/978-1-4899-2271-7

Dooly, M., & O'Dowd, R. (2012). *Researching online foreign language interaction and exchange: theories, methods and challenges. Telecollaboration in Education*. New York: Peter Lang. https://doi.org/10.3726/978-3-0351-0414-1

Dörnyei, Z. (2003). Attitudes, orientations, and motivations in language learning: advances in theory, research, and applications. *Language Learning, 53*(1), 3-32. https://doi.org/10.1111/1467-9922.53222

Dörnyei, Z., & Ushioda, E. (2013). *Teaching and researching: motivation*. Oxford: Routledge.

Gajek, E. (2014). The Effects of Polish-Chinese language tandem work at tertiary level. *US-China Education Review A, 4*(3), 203-208. https://doi.org/10.17265/2161-623X/2014.03A.007

Guth, S., & Helm, F. (2010). *Telecollaboration 2.0: language, literacies and intercultural learning in the 21st century.* New York: Peter Lang. https://doi.org/10.3726/978-3-0351-0013-6

Hall, R. (2009). Towards a fusion of formal and informal learning environments: the impact of the read/write web. *Electronic Journal of e-Learning, 7*(1), 29-40. www.ejel.org/issue/download.html?idArticle=81

Lewis, T., & Walker, L. (Eds). (2003). *Autonomous language learning in tandem.* Sheffield: Academy Electronic Press.

McLoughlin, C., & Lee, M. J. W. (2010). Personalised and self-regulated learning in Web 2. *Australasian Journal of Educational Technology, 26*(1), 28-43. https://doi.org/10.14742/ajet.1100

O'Dowd, R. (Ed.). (2007). *Online intercultural exchange: an introduction for foreign language teachers.* Clevedom: Multilingual Matters.

Pomino, J., & Gil-Salom, D. (2016). Integrating e-tandem in higher education. *Procedia -Social and Behavioral Sciences, 228,* 668-673. https://doi.org/10.1016/j.sbspro.2016.07.102

Ryan, R. M. (1982). Control and information in the intrapersonal sphere: an extension of cognitive evaluation theory. *Journal of Personality and Social Psychology, 43,* 450-461.

Salkind, N. J. (Ed.). (2008). *Encyclopedia of educational psychology.* Thousand Oaks, CA: Sage. https://doi.org/10.4135/9781412963848

Vassallo, M. L., & Telles, J. (2006). Foreign language learning in-tandem: theoretical principles and research perspectives. *The ESPecialist, 27*(1), 83-118. http://www.corpuslg.org/journals/the_especialist/issues/ 27_1_2006/artigo5_Vassalo& Telles.pdf

Voller, P., & Pickard, V. (1996). Conversation exchange: a way towards autonomous language learning. In R. Pemberton, E. S. Li, W. W. Or, & H. D. Pierson (Eds), *Taking control: autonomy in language learning* (pp. 115-132). Hong kong: University Press. http://www.jstor.org/stable/j.ctt2jc12n.15

Wigfield, A., & Eccles, J. (2000). Expectancy–value theory of achievement motivation. *Contemporary Educational Psychology, 25,* 68-81. https://doi.org/10.1006/ceps.1999.1015

12. Informal learning activities for learners of English and for learners of Dutch

Anne Van Marsenille[1]

Abstract

The purpose of this study is to investigate and compare the informal learning activities which French-speaking higher education students in Brussels engage in while learning English and Dutch. The informal learning of English was investigated in 2012, while the informal learning of Dutch was studied in 2015 and then compared to the informal learning of English. The outcomes of this study highlight the importance of raising students' awareness of their informal learning and of raising teachers' awareness of what students do to enhance informal language learning. Teachers may then encourage informal learning by suggesting appropriate materials and methods. The study gives an insight into informal language learning within a formal learning system and the importance of recognising its role therein.

Keywords: English language, Dutch language, informal learning, Brussels.

1. Introduction

This article examines the informal learning of English and Dutch by students at the Institut des Hautes Etudes des Communications Sociales (IHECS), a Higher Education (HE) institution for Communication in Brussels. The aim is to establish what informal language learning activities students engage in and

1. Institut des Hautes Etudes des Communications Sociales, Brussels, Belgium; a.vanmarsenille@gmail.com

How to cite this chapter: Van Marsenille, A. (2017). Informal learning activities for learners of English and for learners of Dutch. In Q. Kan & S. Bax (Eds), *Beyond the language classroom: researching MOOCs and other innovations* (pp. 141-152). Research-publishing.net. https://doi.org/10.14705/rpnet.2017.mooc2016.677

whether the activities differ depending on the learning of English or Dutch. Having first carried out the investigation related to the informal learning of English, I was curious to know if the same activities were used by learners of Dutch. The informal learning of English was investigated in 2012, the informal learning of Dutch was studied in 2015 and then compared to the informal learning of English.

Coffield (2000) observes that although learning is often associated with formal learning institutions, most people tend to learn on an informal basis. He claims that informal learning is as important as formal learning and that it is "fundamental, necessary and valuable in its own right" (p. 8). The Communication from the European Commission (2001, pp. 32-33) differentiates between formal and informal learning. Formal learning is provided by an institution, is structured, and leads to certification. Informal learning results from daily life activities, is not structured and does not lead to certification.

> "As Golding, Brown, and Foley (2008) state, informal language learning has been less examined than formal learning, because it involves many variables. [As] it is not systematic, not organised by an institution and […] is determined by the student, it is harder to identify. […] Being a language teacher and a language learner myself, I notice that much language learning is done outside class" (Van Marsenille, 2015, pp. 9-10).

This investigation studies the views and behaviour of the students at IHECS, a HE institution in Brussels, which is a French/Dutch bilingual city. IHECS offers Bachelor's and Master's degrees in Communication and is a French-medium institution. The learners study Dutch as a second language and English as a foreign language. Dutch is studied as a second language by those for whom it is not the students' mother tongue, but it is a national language of Belgium and one of the official languages in Brussels; English as a foreign language is studied because it is important in the international context and because of the political position of Brussels (Gunderson, D'Silva, & Odo, 2013). In terms of context, the learning of both English and Dutch is important in Belgium, but the situation of each language is very different. English is learnt as an international language, whereas Dutch is learnt as a national language. There is much more material available for learning English as it is studied all over the world, but there are more opportunities to find people speaking Dutch rather than English as their native language in Brussels.

The subdivision of Belgium has an impact on language learning (McGlue, 2003). Belgium is divided into three linguistic communities (French, Flemish, and German) and three regions (the Flemish Region, the Walloon Region, and Brussels-Capital). The Flemish region is officially Dutch-speaking, the Walloon Region mostly French-speaking with a small German-speaking area, and Brussels-Capital is officially bilingual French-Dutch. In Brussels, Dutch is taught as a second language and English as a foreign language.

This study has relevance for students in raising awareness of the importance of informal learning and how it may complement and support formal programmes. It also has relevance for teachers in raising awareness of the activities engaged in by the students in an informal context.

2. Theoretical framework

In this study, I use the definitions given by the European Commission (2001) to examine informal learning, then I look at the context of the informal learning activities related to the learning of English and the learning of Dutch in order to compare one with the other and to relate them to formal learning. The European Commission (2001) differentiates between three types of learning:

> "formal learning that is typically provided by an education or training institution, structured (in terms of learning objectives, learning time or learning support) and that is leading to certification. Formal learning is intentional from the learner's perspective.
>
> Informal learning that results from daily life activities related to work, family or leisure. It is not structured (in terms of learning objectives,

Chapter 12

> learning time or learning support) and typically does not lead to certification. Informal learning may be intentional but in most cases it is non-intentional (or 'incidental'/random).
>
> Non-formal learning that is not provided by an education or training institution and typically does not lead to certification. It is, however, structured (in terms of learning objectives, learning time or learning support). Non-formal learning is intentional from the learner's perspective" (pp. 32-33).

In this study, non-formal learning is not considered. My focus is on informal learning as opposed to formal learning. This difference between formal and informal learning is important as the students involved in this study were taking a formal learning programme. The informal learning activities students engaged in outside their formal programme were investigated because informal learning, which is an important part of language learning, has been less studied than formal learning (Coffield, 2000). As mentioned in Van Marsenille (2015),

> "[a]s far as the location of the learning is concerned, Mahoney (2001) emphasises the fact that formal learning is associated with institutions and focuses on the product or result, whereas informal learning lays the emphasis on the learning process. [...] Informal learning can occur in many different places: at home, at the pub, at the cinema, [or anywhere thanks to the use of mobile devices (Kukulska-Hulme, 2015)]" (p. 27).

The Web can offer the possibility of combining informal and formal learning. Learners watch a lot of TV series on the Internet; the series could be discussed and analysed in class with the teacher or in social media, but some learners prefer their teacher not to interfere in their informal world (Chik & Briedbach, 2014). Chik and Briedbach (2014, p. 113) notices that students use Internet regularly, they also observe that Hong Kong and German students are reading blogs, setting up closed-group learning related Facebook accounts and watching the same TV series.

3. Research questions

The purpose of this study is therefore to investigate which activities students engage in outside the formal setting when learning English and Dutch through the following research questions:

- What type of informal activities do learners of English and Dutch engage in for language learning?

- What are the differences and similarities between learners of English and learners of Dutch in their informal learning activities?

4. Method

4.1. Research participants

In the first part of the study in 2012, 80 students from four classes (20 from each class, two classes in the second year and two classes in the third year) were invited to complete a questionnaire related to the informal learning of English. In the second part of the study in 2015, 80 different students from four classes (same number per class and same year groups as above) completed the same questionnaire about informal learning of Dutch. This number of participants represents one-fifth of the active student population for both the second and the third year for each language cohort. Two-thirds of the participants in the sample were female, which was representative of the student population at IHECS. They were between 20 and 22 years old. The main reason for choosing these two year groups is that in the second and third year, students are learning general vocabulary and grammar of the foreign and second language.

4.2. Data collection and analysis

A questionnaire was used in order to collect quantitative data regarding participants' background and informal activities for language learning. As all the participants' first language was French, the questionnaire was given in French to avoid potential misunderstandings. The questionnaire includes alternative sections which were used in the first and second part of the study depending on whether participants were studying English or Dutch[2].

The data from the questionnaires were analysed by creating a spreadsheet in Excel for the different responses related to the themes in the questionnaire. For each informal activity, the participants were asked to indicate the frequency by choosing 'Very often', 'Often', 'Occasionally' or 'Never'. The percentage frequency was calculated for each informal learning activity. Comparisons of frequencies were made between learners of English and Dutch.

5. Findings

The numbers in brackets show the actual number of responses out of the total (80 from learners of English, 80 from learners of Dutch). The findings will be presented after the table.

Table 1. Informal learning activities for learners of English ($N=80$) and Dutch ($N=80$)

Informal learning	in ENGLISH				in DUTCH			
	Very often	Often	Occasionally	Never	Very often	Often	Occasionally	Never
No 1. reading newspaper and/or magazine articles	10% (8)	31% (25)	53% (42)	6% (5)	4% (3)	20% (16)	58% (46)	18% (15)
No 2. reading books	4% (3)	14% (11)	64% (51)	18% (14)	0% (0)	2% (2)	20% (16)	78% (62)
No 3. reading webpages (e.g. blogs, reports)	30% (24)	38% (30)	29% (23)	4% (3)	4% (3)	26% (21)	52% (42)	18% (14)
No 4. watching local television programmes	23% (18)	15% (12)	31% (25)	31% (25)	10% (8)	12% (10)	50% (40)	28% (22)

2. English versions of the full questionnaires are available from the author.

Activity								
No 5. watching films and/or TV series online	58% (46)	35% (28)	8% (6)	0% (0)	2% (2)	8% (6)	36% (29)	54% (43)
No 6. watching documentaries	11% (9)	21% (17)	36% (29)	31% (25)	2% (2)	2% (2)	32% (25)	64% (51)
No 7. listening to the radio	1% (1)	3% (2)	26% (21)	70% (56)	12% (10)	18% (14)	42% (34)	30% (24)
No 8. writing to students and/or penfriend	10% (8)	11% (9)	19% (15)	60% (48)	0% (0)	12% (10)	26% (21)	62% (49)
No 9. writing on the web	18% (14)	16% (13)	36% (29)	30% (24)	4% (3)	6% (5)	28% (22)	62% (50)
No 10. speaking to English-speaking people/Dutch-speaking people in Brussels	8% (6)	8% (6)	61% (49)	23% (19)	10% (8)	20% (16)	60% (48)	10% (8)
No 11. speaking to English-speaking people in other countries	16% (13)	39% (31)	40% (32)	5% (4)	-	-	-	-
No 12. going to Flanders (Dutch-speaking Northern region of Belgium)	-	-	-	-	12% (10)	16% (13)	62% (50)	10% (8)
No 13. going to the Netherlands	-	-	-	-	4% (3)	10% (8)	68% (55)	18% (14)
No 14. participating in cultural events	0% (0)	6% (5)	34% (27)	60% (48)	-	-	-	-
No 15. going to Flemish events	-	-	-	-	2% (1)	8% (6)	42% (33)	50% (40)
No 16. going to events with Dutch-speaking people	-	-	-	-	2% (2)	12% (10)	32% (25)	54% (43)
No 17. going to the pub and speaking Dutch	-	-	-	-	2% (2)	6% (5)	26% (21)	66% (52)

5.1. Similarities

Looking at the similarities in the learning of English and Dutch, the results suggest that students learning English and Dutch tend to engage in the following informal learning activities: a little over 50% of the participants for both groups occasionally read newspapers and magazines (No 1); and 60% for both groups occasionally speak to English-speaking people or Dutch-speaking people in Brussels (No 10). Regarding writing to students and/or penfriends, a high proportion of participants (over 60%) in both languages never engage in this activity.

5.2. Differences

The main differences between the activities for students of English and Dutch are:

- 93% of the participants learning English watch films and TV series (mainly online) outside class (No 5) and 64% occasionally read books (No 2), but 54% of participants learning Dutch never watch films and/or TV series (No 5), and 78% of participants learning Dutch never read books (No 2). It is because there is a large offer of films, TV series and books in English, but for Dutch the offer is limited. Another explanation might be that students read Internet pages; traditional paper books are not so popular nowadays.

- 70% of participants learning English never listen to the radio (No 7), whereas this is the case for only 30% of participants learning Dutch (No 7). Nowadays, students would rather listen to podcasts or audio clips instead of radio programmes. This is probably the reason why 70% of the learners of English never listen to the radio and 30% of the learners of Dutch never listen to radio programmes.

- More participants learning Dutch (50%) than those learning English (31%) occasionally watch local television programmes (No 4). In Belgium, there is a larger offer of Flemish (national) television and radio programmes than of English language programmes.

- It is natural that speaking to people and participating in cultural events is done more by students learning Dutch as they can take advantage of the surrounding environment. It is also easier for students learning Dutch than for students learning English to go to the neighbouring region or country and speak the language; indeed, there is no neighbouring country where students could speak English with the locals. 62% of students learning Dutch occasionally go to Flanders (No 12) and 68% of students learning Dutch occasionally go to the Netherlands (No 13). Although English is spoken in many countries as a national language or as a lingua franca, the countries where English is spoken are further from Brussels than the places where Dutch is spoken; it requires more effort to go to English-speaking countries.

6. Discussion of the findings

This article has shed light on how students learn informally and on how this may differ according to the language the students are learning. As far as I am aware, there has not been another study comparing English learners with Dutch learners in terms of informal activities for language learning set in a higher education institution in Brussels.

In line with Van Marsenille (2015), this study has shown that students of English spend quite a lot of time watching films and TV series in English. Watching films and TV series on the Internet is a popular activity for young people nowadays. Belgian students watch the same TV series as other students from different countries in the world do and they share their views about them on the Internet (Chik & Briedbach, 2014). These widespread TV series and movies offer material to learn English and to discuss in English with people around the world. My data suggests that students do that very often.

As far as the learning of Dutch is concerned, only 8% of participants often watch films in Dutch (No 5). This is because the offer in Dutch is limited. Dutch is a local language, whereas English is an international language.

As far as location is concerned, informal learning can occur in different places (Lafraya, 2012, p. 11). Learners of English tend to engage in activities for English learning on an informal basis mostly through the Internet, 58% of participants learning English very often watch films and TV series on the

Internet (No 5); whereas students of Dutch participate more in real-life activities, 20% of participants learning Dutch often speak to locals in Brussels and 60% of participants learning Dutch occasionally do so (No 10).

Young language learners in general use the Internet very often and also for other purposes (Chik & Briedbach, 2014): they listen to music, they read blogs – 38% of participants learning English often do so and 52% of participants learning Dutch occasionally do so (No3).

54% of participants learning Dutch never go to events with Dutch-speaking people in Brussels (No 16). It is probably because they have opportunities to meet Dutch-speaking people (20% often speak to Dutch-speaking people), as Brussels is bilingual French and Dutch. Flanders and the Netherlands are close to Brussels. Learners of Dutch do not use the opportunities they have close to the place they study to their full extent, especially as they do not often take part in events in Dutch. They do not make full use of 'the world as a classroom' (Coleman & Baumann, 2005).

As discussed in Van Marsenille (2015), "this investigation should help […] raise awareness of some of the informal learning activities [engaged in] by HE language students, so that teachers can take them into account in their formal learning [context]" (p. 165). If teachers know what students do outside class as far as the learning of the language is concerned, they may link this to activities in class so as to motivate students to learn more on an informal basis. This can help bridge the gap between both types of learning and give importance to informal learning, which should be recognised as being as important as formal learning, as Coffield (2000) stated.

7. Conclusion

Currently, there appears to be a gap between informal and formal learning because class activities, such as reading and discussing a newspaper article or listening to the news, are not directly related to the student's informal learning activities.

At the IHECS where I am currently teaching, teachers report that they do not know much about their students' informal learning activities and that they do not consider discussing them in the formal class. As stated elsewhere, "[i]f students and teachers [knew] more about the different informal learning activities [available to learners], they could make better use of them; the activities could be taken into account in the formal learning programme" (Van Marsenille, 2015, p. 182).

A limitation of this study is that the reasons for engaging in the informal learning activities were not explored. This investigation will be followed up by interviews to further investigate informal learning activities and the reasons for engaging in them.

The study nevertheless gives an insight into informal language learning adjacent to a formal learning system and the importance of recognising its role. The data indicates that students engage in a wide range of informal activities to support their language learning. Although teachers in the formal learning framework can help the student learn on an informal basis, some learners may not want their teacher to interfere in their informal world. They prefer to create their own Facebook group (Chik & Briedbach, 2014) without the guidance of the teacher. So how can teachers support informal language learning without students feeling that their space is being invaded? Further research will be needed to help us better understand the teacher's role in informal settings as well as formal settings.

References

Chik, A., & Briedbach, S. (2014). 'Facebook me' within a global community of learners of English: technologizing learner autonomy. In G. Murray (Ed.), *Social dimensions of autonomy in language learning* (pp. 100-118). London: Palgrave Macmillan. https://doi.org/10.1057/9781137290243_6

Coffield, F. (Ed.). (2000). *The necessity of informal learning.* Bristol: The Policy Press.

Coleman, J., & Baumann, U. (2005). The world as a classroom. In S. Hurd & L. Murphy (Eds), *Success with languages* (pp. 140-160). Abingdon, Oxon: Routledge.

European Commission. (2001). *Communication from the Commission: making a European area of lifelong learning a reality.* Brussels. .

Golding, B., Brown, M., & Foley, A. (2008). Informal learning: a discussion around defining and researching its breadth and importance. In B. Golding, M. Brown, & A. Foley (Eds), *Adult learning Australia Conference, 48th, 2008, Perth, WA.*

Gunderson, L., D'Silva, R. A., & Odo, D. M. (Eds). (2013). *ESL (ELL) literacy instruction: a guidebook to theory and practice.* New York: Routledge.

Kukulska-Hulme, A. (2015). Language as a bridge connecting formal and informal language learning through mobile devices. In L.-H. Wong, M. Milrad, & M. Specht (Eds), *Seamless learning in the age of mobile connectivity* (pp. 281-294). Singapore: Springer. https://doi.org/10.1007/978-981-287-113-8_14

Lafraya, S. (2012). *Intercultural learning in non-formal education: theoretical frameworks and starting points.* Council of Europe ed. Strasburg: Council of Europe Publishing.

Mahoney, J. (2001). What is informal education? In L. D. Richardson & M. Wolfe (Eds), *Principles and practice of informal education: learning through life* (pp. 17-33). Abingdon, Oxon: RoutledgeFalmer.

McGlue, H. (2003). *Language issues: where does one observe language to be a problem in the country?* Brussels: Eurolang News.

Van Marsenille, A. (2015). *Informal language learning: the perspective of higher education students in Brussels. A case dtudy.* Doctoral thesis. The Open University.

Author index

A
Altamimi, Shooq v, 3, 71

B
Bax, Stephen v, 1
Beaven, Tita vi, 3, 127
Bekaryan, Lilit vi, 3, 113
Bellassen, Joël vi, 3, 43

C
Conde Gafaro, Barbara vi, 3, 71

D
Demeulenaere, Kathy vii, 3, 29
De Waard, Inge vii, 2, 29

F
Fuertes Gutiérrez, Mara vii, 3, 127

H
Harutyunyan, Arusyak vii, 3, 113

K
Kan, Qian v, 1

M
Magnoni, Francesca vii, 3, 59
Mason, Amanda viii, 3, 99
McLoughlin, Laura viii, 3, 59
Motzo, Anna viii, 3, 85, 127

O
Orsini-Jones, Marina viii, 3, 71

P
Proudfoot, Anna ix, 3, 85

S
Soghomonyan, Zaruhi ix, 3, 113

T
Troncarelli, Donatella ix, 2, 5

V
Van Marsenille, Anne ix, 3, 141
Villarini, Andrea x, 2, 5

W
Wang-Szilas, Jue x, 3, 43

Z
Zhang, Wenxin x, 3, 99
Zhang, Xinying x, 2, 15

www.ingramcontent.com/pod-product-compliance
Lightning Source LLC
Chambersburg PA
CBHW031147160426
43193CB00008B/283